INDIAN FOOD UNDER PRESSURE

ASHLEY SINGH THOMAS
OF **MY HEART BEETS**

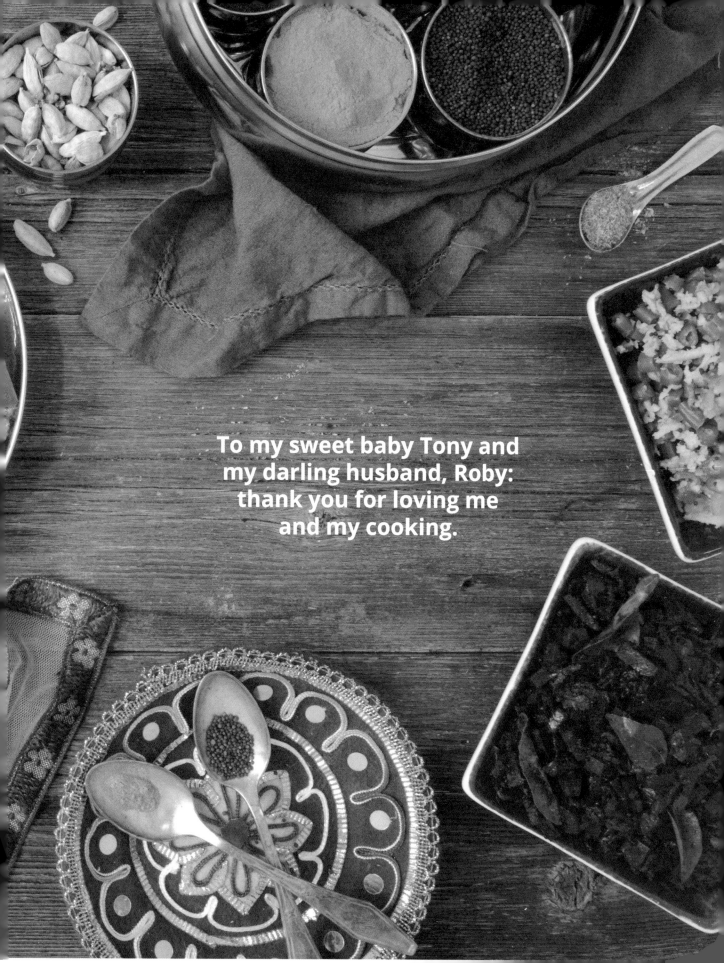

To my sweet baby Tony and
my darling husband, Roby:
thank you for loving me
and my cooking.

CONTENTS

ASHLEY SINGH THOMAS

Hello! I'm Ashley, the founder of My Heart Beets, a blog dedicated to flavorful, real food recipes. Even though I share a variety of recipes on my website, Indian cuisine is easily my favorite.

I grew up in an Indian household eating delicious North Indian food, and I was completely unaware of how varied Indian cuisine was until I started dating Roby. He introduced me to South Indian cuisine, specifically Keralite food, and I fell in love (with both him and the food).

It wasn't until I got married that I really felt the desire to learn my family's recipes. The problem was that when I'd call to ask for measurements, my mom would tell me she cooks "andaz naal" which basically means she eyeballs everything. Most Indian parents don't measure ingredients (ever) and so trying to recreate recipes was really tough. Whenever I'd visit home, I'd follow my parents and my in-laws around the kitchen, taking notes and asking questions. I would sometimes "help" them as they cooked, measuring their ingredients before they threw them into the pot. I also started paying close attention to ratios as well as how things were supposed to taste. I used this information, gathered over several years, to test and develop many of the recipes that I share both on my blog and also in my books. For this particular cookbook, I have adapted all recipes to be electric pressure cooker friendly.

This book features both North and South Indian recipes. If you enjoy eating at Indian restaurants, then you'll be happy to know I've included recipes for many dishes commonly found on restaurant menus. I'm obviously biased but I believe my recipes are just as good, if not better than restaurant-quality. There may be some unfamiliar recipes in this book too. I hope you'll try them as they are equally delicious.

And finally, if you do like this book and want to try more recipes or want to learn a little more about me, I hope you'll visit my blog, MyHeartBeets.com.

HOW TO USE THIS BOOK
10 THINGS TO KNOW
BEFORE YOU START COOKING

1 All Multicookers Vary: I own two different electric pressure cookers and there are slight differences between them. For example, one has a "manual" button and the other does not. In most of my recipes, once you are done with the "sauté" portion, you will need to press another button to begin the actual pressure cooking. All pressure cookers vary and so you may find that you need to slightly adjust the recipe instructions and cook times in this book. Make sure to read the instruction manual that came with your appliance.

2 Read Recipes in Entirety: Make sure to read through the recipes before you begin cooking so that there aren't any surprises halfway through.

3 Gather Spices: Taking a minute to gather and measure all of the spices listed in a recipe before you begin can make a huge difference in the outcome of your dish. If you're not prepared, you'll be searching for spices and adding them to the pot one at a time which will most definitely cause your spices to burn.

4 Prepare Ingredients: I know I specifically called out spices right before this because I believe that's crucial, but I also think it's a good idea to prepare the rest of the ingredients beforehand as well. Dice onions, mince garlic, etc. Better yet, keep a jar of minced garlic or minced ginger in the fridge or freezer (I add a little oil to keep the garlic and ginger fresh). This will ensure that cooking goes smoothly.

5 Adjust to Taste: While you can't substitute everything in a recipe and expect it to taste as it should, there are some instances when you can and should adapt a recipe to suit your tastes. Feel free to change the amount of salt or chilies used in any recipe in this book. If you like your food on the saltier side, add more salt. If you want to enjoy spicier food, add more cayenne or extra green chilies. I personally like Serrano peppers, but you can use bird's eye chili or jalapeños or whatever you want. I prefer my food slightly spicy, but my husband prefers his food ridiculously spicy, so he adds fresh green chilies or extra cayenne directly to his bowl. You can also adjust the consistency of a dish. If you prefer a thicker sauce, press the sauté button when your dish is done to reduce the gravy. Likewise, you can add water to create a thinner curry.

6 Use fresh ingredients: Old beans take longer to cook. Fresh spices have more flavor. I try to buy whole spices when I can and grind them in a spice grinder for maximum flavor.

7 Oil: I typically use avocado oil in most of my recipes because it's a very neutral oil, but you can use any neutral oil you like. If I specify a certain type of fat (coconut oil or ghee), then try to use it because the flavor will add to the dish.

8 Size Doesn't Really Matter: When it comes to cooking Indian food, the size of the tomato or the onion you use isn't going to make or break a recipe, so don't sweat it. I intentionally did not write "medium" or "large" before most ingredients because I know the majority of people don't care to measure the diameter of a tomato. When I was new to cooking, I used to really worry about this so I'm sure there are some of you who might be in that position too. What I've learned after years of cooking Indian food is that it honestly does not matter. If you like onions, use a large onion.

9 Kashmiri Chili: Long-time readers of my blog (My Heart Beets) know that I used to use Kashmiri chili in my recipes. Kashmiri chili has a very mild flavor (it's not spicy at all). It's kind of like (sweet) paprika with a very light touch of cayenne. If you want to use Kashmiri chili then feel free to use it as a replacement for paprika.

10 Have Questions About a Recipe? I want to help you. My goal with this book is to make Indian cooking more approachable. Feel free to email me at Ashley@MyHeartBeets.com. Please keep in mind that in addition to being a blogger, I'm also a full-time mom, so it may take me time to reply.

WHY COOK INDIAN FOOD WITH AN ELECTRIC PRESSURE COOKER?

I have been using an electric pressure cooker for several years now, but it wasn't until I became a mother that this appliance became my go-to cooking device. I have been able to adapt so many Indian recipes to be one-pot friendly, making the recipes much more approachable. I use my pressure cooker daily, sometimes multiple times a day, and when it comes to Indian cooking this is pretty much the only appliance I use these days.

5 REASONS WHY I LOVE COOKING (INDIAN) FOOD WITH AN ELECTRIC PRESSURE COOKER:

1 **No Need to Babysit:** When you cook your meal on the stovetop, be it in a regular pot or a traditional pressure cooker, you need to heat it over a burner and watch it closely. However, with an electric pressure cooker, you just plug it in, press a button and let it do the rest.

2 **Traps Aroma and Flavor:** I'll be honest, by "aroma," I mean "smell." I love Indian food, but those of us who cook it often know that the scent of ginger, garlic, onion and spices can seep into everything around the kitchen. While I don't mind the smell of onion and garlic, I don't necessarily want my clothes, jackets and everything on the first floor to smell. In my opinion, the pressure cooker does a much better job at containing that smell. I've also noticed that the pressure cooker makes food more flavorful; spices seem to infuse better than they do when I'm cooking on the stovetop.

3 One Pot, Less Mess: I love how easy it is to clean an electric pressure cooker! I just put my steel insert into the dishwasher, which is something I can't do with most of my pots and pans. That said, I do suggest keeping two silicone rings on hand: one for savory recipes and one for sweet recipes. No matter how hard you try to keep your silicone ring clean, the fact is that it will absorb strong flavors.

4 Reliable: Using an electric pressure cooker provides consistent results because there's less room for human error. I get distracted easily, especially while caring for my baby. When I'm cooking on the stovetop, I have to keep track of time, whereas with an electric pressure cooker that isn't an issue. Heat evenly distributes and cooks the food perfectly. Each time I make a dish, I can expect it to turn out the same.

5 Good Food Ready Fast*: The reason this comes with an asterisk is because the truth is, it's not always faster to cook food in a pressure cooker, especially when it comes to quick cooking meats and vegetables. That's one reason I chose not to include seafood recipes in this cookbook. This appliance takes time to build pressure before the cook time begins and it also takes time to naturally release pressure once the cook time is over. When it comes to cooking legumes or other meat, especially red meat, it is certainly faster to use an electric pressure cooker than to use a regular pot over the stove. You might be wondering if a stovetop pressure cooker is a faster option? While a stovetop pressure cooker is technically slightly faster in terms of cook time, I think that once you take into account the amount of time and effort spent watching over it, counting whistles and hand washing the parts, that it's actually easier and faster to cook food in an electric pressure cooker.

DINNER MENU IDEAS

HERE IS SOME INSPIRATION TO GET YOU STARTED!

Friends and blog readers often ask me what dishes to pair together when creating a menu. While there are no set rules, I typically aim to serve dishes that differ in taste and texture. I try to pair a "wet" dish (e.g. Butter Chicken) with a "dry" dish (e.g. Cabbage and Peas).

If you're planning to prepare a proper Indian meal, I suggest serving these items with each menu: plain basmati rice, naan, salad, raita (yogurt mixed with a little water, salt and roasted cumin powder), Indian pickles/chutney.

FANCY DINNER PARTY MENU

Chicken Biryani
Tangy Tomato & Fresh Corn Soup
Spiced Buttery Lentils DAL MAKHANI
Potato & Eggplant in Pickling Spices ACHARI ALOO BAINGAN
Creamy Cardamom Rice Pudding KHEER

WEEKNIGHT MENU

Spiced Ground Meat and Rice KEEMA PULAO
Yellow Lentils with Spinach PALAK MOONG DAL
Cabbage and Peas

VEGAN MENU

Vegetable Korma*
Masala Dal
Potato & Eggplant in Pickling Spices ACHARI ALOO BAINGAN
Carrot Pudding GAJAR KA HALWA*
*Substitute ghee with coconut oil and heavy cream with coconut milk

VEGETARIAN MENU

Masala Egg Roast   NADAN MUTTA ROAST
Lentils in Coconut Curry   KERALA PARIPPU
Mushrooms in an Onion Gravy   MUSHROOM DO PYAZA
Butternut Squash Pudding   HALWA

KERALITE MENU

Kerala Beef Fry   ERACHI ULARTHIYATHU
Coconut Rice
Beet Stir-fry   BEET THORAN
Mixed Vegetables in Yogurt Sauce   AVIAL
Sweet Lentils in Coconut Milk   MOONG DAL PAYASAM

PUNJABI MENU

Butter Chicken   MURGH MAKHANI
Spiced Chickpea Curry   CHOLE/CHANA MASALA
Potatoes and Cauliflower   ALOO GOBI
Spiced Buttery Greens   SAAG
Carrot Pudding   GAJAR KA HALWA

BRUNCH MENU

Steamed Rice Cakes   IDLI
or Crispy Crepes   DOSA
Split Pea & Vegetable Soup   SAMBAR
Spiced Brown Chickpeas   SUKHE KALA CHANA MASALA
Sweet Saffron Fruit & Nut Rice   MEETHE CHAWAL
Chai

MEAT MASALA
(SOUTH INDIAN GARAM MASALA)

There is a big difference between the garam masala used in North India and in South India. The garam masala that you find in most grocery stores is a North Indian blend which is why I am sharing a recipe for South Indian Garam Masala, also known as Meat Masala. I share both North Indian and South Indian recipes in this book, and in order for a dish to taste as it should, you'll want to use the right type of garam masala. If a recipe calls for "Meat Masala" then please use this blend and know that you're making a South Indian (to be specific, a Keralite) dish.

4 full tablespoons green cardamom pods

3 tablespoons whole cloves

3 sticks or pieces of cinnamon or cassia

½ cup fennel seeds

1 tablespoon whole black peppercorns

1 whole nutmeg

Heat a skillet over low heat and dry roast all of the spices for 5-10 minutes, stirring occasionally to toast all sides of the spices. Turn off the heat and allow the spices to cool. Remove the whole nutmeg from the pan and cut it into small pieces, then place it into a spice grinder along with the rest of the whole spices. Grind the spices until mostly smooth. Store in an airtight jar and use within 6-8 months for the most flavor.

ROASTED CUMIN POWDER
(BHUNA JEERA POWDER)

Roasted cumin powder is highly aromatic and has a more intense flavor than regular (unroasted) cumin. It's slightly nutty and adds a unique flavor to recipes. If a recipe calls for roasted cumin powder, do not substitute it with regular cumin as you won't get the right flavor. You can sprinkle this directly onto a dish or onto yogurt for more flavor.

1 cup cumin seeds (or desired amount)

Heat a skillet over low heat and dry roast the cumin seeds for 5-10 minutes, stirring occasionally until the color of the cumin changes to a dark brown. Turn off the heat and allow the cumin seeds to cool down. Place the cumin into a spice grinder and blend until smooth. Store in an airtight jar and use within 6-8 months for the most flavor.

RICE
& DAL

KIDNEY
BEANS

SPLIT AND SKINLESS
BLACK LENTILS
(SPLIT AND SKINLESS
URAD DAL)

SPLIT PIGEON PEAS
(TOOR DAL)

RED LENTILS
(MASOOR DAL)

WHOLE SKINLESS
BLACK LENTILS
(WHOLE SKINLESS
URAD DAL)

SMALL
YELLOW LENTILS
(MOONG DAL)

WHOLE MUNG BEANS

BLACK-EYED PEAS

CHICKPEAS

WHOLE BLACK LENTILS (WHOLE URAD DAL)

SPLIT CHICKPEAS (CHANA DAL)

BROWN CHICKPEAS (KALA CHANA)

BASMATI
RICE

Serves 2-3

Basmati rice is an aromatic long grain rice that has a slightly nutty flavor to it. You can tell when this type of rice is cooked properly because the grains don't stick together. I suggest soaking the rice in cold water because it allows the rice to absorb some water which helps keep it soft and it also helps reduce starch which can make the rice sticky. There are several types of basmati rice and so you may have to adjust the time according to the brand you use. I typically use organic basmati rice or Aahu Barah basmati rice (our favorite!) and the method below results in perfectly cooked rice.

1 cup basmati rice,
  soaked for 15-30 minutes

1 tablespoon oil of choice

1 cup water

½ teaspoon salt,
  adjust to taste

1.   Soak the basmati rice in cold water for 15-30 minutes. Drain, rinse and set aside.

2.   Press the sauté button and allow the pot to heat up for a minute. Then add the oil and swirl it around the pot. This will help ensure that the rice doesn't stick. Add the rice, water and salt to the pot and mix well.

3.   Secure the lid, close the pressure valve and cook for 6 minutes at high pressure.

4.   Naturally release pressure for 10 minutes. Open the valve to release any remaining pressure.

5.   Fluff the rice with a fork and serve.

PEA PULAO

MATAR PULAO

Serves 2-3

This mildly flavored rice dish, also known as matar pulao, is so easy to make. The caramelized onions, aromatic spices and the sweetness from the peas make this bowl of rice taste a little extra special.

1 cup basmati rice,
   soaked for 15-30 minutes

3 tablespoons oil of choice

1 teaspoon cumin seeds

3 green cardamom pods

2 whole cloves

1 bay leaf

½ cinnamon stick

½ onion, diced

1 cup fresh or frozen green peas

1 cup water

½ teaspoon salt

1. Soak the basmati rice in cold water for 15-30 minutes. Drain, rinse and set aside.

2. Press the sauté button, add the oil and allow it to heat up for a minute. Add the cumin seeds and once they begin to brown, add the cardamom, cloves, bay leaf and cinnamon stick. Give everything a quick stir, then add the diced onion.

3. Stir-fry for 6-7 minutes, or until the onion begins to brown. Then add the rice, peas, water and salt. Mix well.

4. Secure the lid, close the pressure valve and cook for 6 minutes at high pressure.

5. Naturally release pressure for 10 minutes. Open the valve to release any remaining pressure.

6. Fluff the rice with a fork and serve.

LEMON
RICE

Serves 3-4

This popular South Indian rice dish is light, tangy and refreshing. The citrus flavor in the rice really comes through. You can eat this for breakfast, as a snack or as part of a meal. I enjoy eating lemon rice with a side of yogurt and Indian pickles.

1 cup basmati rice,
  soaked for 15-30 minutes

3 tablespoons oil of choice

1 teaspoon black mustard seeds

1 tablespoon split chickpeas
  (chana dal)

1 tablespoon split and skinless black lentils
  (split and skinless urad dal)

⅓ cup raw peanuts*

15 curry leaves

1 Serrano pepper or green chili, slit but intact

1 teaspoon minced ginger

1 teaspoon coriander powder

1 teaspoon salt

½ teaspoon turmeric

¼ cup lemon juice

2 teaspoons lemon zest, optional

1 cup water

1. Soak the basmati rice in cold water for 15-30 minutes. Drain the water, rinse and set aside.

2. Press the sauté button, add the oil and allow it to heat up for a minute. Add the mustard seeds, split chickpeas, split/skinless black lentils. After 1-2 minutes, or once the lentils turn golden in color, add the raw peanuts and stir-fry.

3. Add the curry leaves, Serrano pepper, ginger, coriander powder, salt and turmeric. Stir-fry for 30 seconds, then add lemon juice, lemon zest, water and rice. Mix well.

4. Secure the lid, close the pressure valve and cook for 6 minutes at high pressure.

5. Naturally release pressure for 10 minutes. Open the valve to release any remaining pressure.

6. Fluff the rice with a fork and serve.

*I prefer using raw peanuts in this dish, which can easily be found at any Indian grocery store or online. You can use roasted peanuts or cashews instead, just wait to add them in with the spices.

COCONUT
RICE

This is one of my favorite ways to make rice. The grated coconut makes this dish so fluffy and the curry leaves add great flavor. While freshly grated coconut would taste amazing in this dish, I always use frozen grated coconut (unsweetened), available in the frozen section of your local Indian grocery store.

Serves 3-4

1 cup basmati rice,
   soaked for 15-30 minutes

2 tablespoons coconut oil

1 teaspoon black mustard seeds

1 tablespoon split chickpeas
   (chana dal)

1 tablespoon split and skinless black lentils
   (split and skinless urad dal)

15 curry leaves

15 cashews, split in half

1 Serrano pepper or green chili,
   slit but still intact

2 cups frozen, grated coconut*

1 ½ cups water

1 teaspoon salt

1. Soak the basmati rice in cold water for 15-30 minutes. Drain, rinse and set aside.

2. Press the sauté button, and add the coconut oil. Once it melts, add the mustard seeds, split chickpeas, split/skinless black lentils. Once the mustard seeds begin to pop and the lentils turn golden in color, add the curry leaves, cashews and Serrano pepper. Stir for 30 seconds.

3. Add the coconut and stir for another 30 seconds, then add the rice, water and salt. Mix well.

4. Secure the lid, close the pressure valve and cook for 6 minutes at high pressure.

5. Naturally release pressure for 10 minutes. Open the valve to release any remaining pressure.

6. Fluff the rice with a fork, and serve.

*Find frozen unsweetened grated coconut at your local Indian grocery store.

IDLI & DOSA **BATTER**

This batter is made up of rice and lentils and can be used to make soft steamed rice patties or crispy crepes. You can store the batter in your fridge for about a week or in the freezer for about a month. Use the batter to make idlis the first couple days, then use the batter to make crispy dosas or savory "pancakes" the rest of the week. One note, be sure to use rice that is labeled "Idli rice" when making this recipe. Idli rice is short grain parboiled rice and can be easily found at any Indian grocery store or on Amazon.

3 cups idli rice
  (short grain parboiled rice),
  soaked for 5-6 hours

1 cup whole skinless black lentils
  (whole skinless urad dal),
  soaked for 5-6 hours

1 teaspoon fenugreek (methi) seeds,
  soaked for 5-6 hours

2 cups cold water,
  adjust accordingly

3 teaspoons salt

Soak the rice and lentils in the morning so you can prepare the batter in the evening and allow it to ferment overnight.

1.   To prepare the batter, soak the rice in a bowl of cold water for 5-6 hours. In a separate bowl, add the whole skinless black lentils (urad dal) and fenugreek seeds and soak in cold water for 5-6 hours. Drain the water.

2.   Put the drained rice in a blender and slowly pour in 1 cup of cold water while blending. Blend until the rice is mostly smooth. Pour this into the steel pot. Add the drained urad dal and methi seeds to the blender and slowly pour the in remaining 1 cup of cold water while blending. Blend until the dal is a fluffy, almost foam-like consistency. Pour this into the steel inner pot. Mix the blended rice and dal together.

3.   Press the yogurt button and set the time to 12 hours on normal mode. Secure the lid. You can close the valve or leave it open as it does not matter in this case. Once the time is up, the batter should have doubled in size and look light and airy. Gently fold the salt into the batter.

4.   Store the batter in the fridge for up to a week, or keep it in the freezer for up to a month.

STEAMED RICE CAKES

IDLI

These rice and lentil cakes are typically served with sambar or chutney during breakfast or lunch. Idli is typically eaten in savory applications, but you can also top them with ghee and sugar (my husband's favorite way to eat them).

Idli & Dosa Batter

1.   To make idlis, spoon the fermented batter into a greased idli mold.

2.   Place 2 cups of water into the steel inner pot, then place the idli mold inside the pot.

3.   Secure the lid, close the pressure valve and cook for 1 minute at high pressure (the idlis will cook while the machine builds pressure).

4.   Naturally release pressure for 10 minutes. Open the valve to release any remaining pressure.

5.   Serve with sambar.

THIN & CRISPY
CREPES
DOSA

A dosa is similar to a crepe or a pancake and can vary in thickness. I prefer to make thin, crispy dosas using the recipe below. If you have trouble spreading out the batter to make thin dosas or just feel like trying something new then try making something called uttapam, which is basically just a thicker dosa with toppings cooked into it. To make uttapam, follow the steps below but instead of oil, sprinkle the flatbread with chopped onions, tomatoes and green chilies before you flip it over to cook the other side.

1 cup Idli & dosa batter (pg 16)

1 tablespoon chickpea flour

1 teaspoon sugar

2-4 tablespoons water

Oil of choice

1. To make dosa, pour 1 cup of idli/dosa batter into a bowl along with the chickpea flour and sugar. Mix until well combined.

2. Slowly add 1 tablespoon of water at a time until the batter is slightly runny.

3. Heat a well-seasoned or non-stick crepe pan over high heat, then ladle the batter onto the pan and spread it around the pan slowly.

4. The edges of the dosa will lift from the pan when the bottom side is done. Sprinkle a few drops of oil on top of the bread, then flip the dosa over to cook the other side for 30 seconds.

5. Serve dosa with sambar.

SPLIT PIGEON PEA & VEGETABLE
SOUP
SAMBAR

This tamarind flavored lentil and vegetable stew is a very popular South Indian dish. It almost always accompanies idli or dosa.

Serves 3-4

1 cup split pigeon peas (toor dal), soaked for 1 hour

1 tablespoon oil of choice

½ teaspoon black mustard seeds

¼ teaspoon fenugreek (methi) seeds

15 curry leaves

1 teaspoon minced garlic

1 teaspoon minced ginger

SPICES

2 teaspoons coriander powder

2 teaspoon salt, adjust to taste

1 teaspoon paprika

½ teaspoon turmeric powder

¼ teaspoon black pepper

¼ teaspoon cayenne

¼ teaspoon roasted cumin powder (pg 8)

4 cups water

3 cups chopped mixed vegetables*

1 tomato, chopped

½ onion, chopped into chunks

1 teaspoon sugar

1 teaspoon tamarind paste

*This dish is typically made with mixed vegetables like okra, eggplant, carrots, green beans, potatoes and drumsticks. You can find drumsticks, also known as moringa, in the frozen aisle of any Indian grocery store. When eating drumsticks, eat the inside and then discard the fibrous exterior.

1.   Soak the split pigeon peas (toor dal) in cold water for 1 hour. Drain, rinse and set aside.

2.   Press the sauté button, add the oil and allow it to heat up for a minute. Add the mustard seeds and fenugreek seeds. Once the mustard seeds begin to splutter, add the curry leaves, garlic, ginger and spices. Stir, then add the remaining ingredients and mix well.

3.   Secure the lid, close the pressure valve and cook for 10 minutes at high pressure.

4.   Naturally release pressure for 15 minutes. Open the valve to release any remaining pressure.

5.   Serve over rice or with idli or dosa.

RICE AND LENTIL
PORRIDGE

KHICHDI

Serves 4-5

In many Indian households, this dish is often prepared for the very young, the sick and the elderly. When I came home from the hospital after giving birth to Tony, my mom made me this porridge every day for a week (along with other healing foods) because it's thought to be easy on the stomach. Khichdi is prepared slightly differently depending on what region you're from in India. Below is the way my family makes this dish: with a few simple spices and plenty of ghee. This recipe is easily customizable, so feel free to add ginger, garlic, green chilies or more spices if you wish. You can also make this porridge as thick or as thin as you'd like. If you prefer a thinner consistency, just add more water at the end. I always top my bowl with a spoonful of ghee and a pinch of salt before serving.

1 cup basmati rice,
   soaked for 15-30 minutes

½ cup small yellow lentils
   (moong dal), soaked for
   15-30 minutes

2 tablespoons ghee
   or oil of choice

1 ½ teaspoons cumin seeds

1 bay leaf

6 cups water

1 ½ teaspoons salt

1 teaspoon turmeric

Ghee, for serving

1. Soak the basmati rice and small yellow lentils (moong dal) in cold water for 15-30 minutes. Drain, rinse and set aside.

2. Press the sauté button, then add the ghee or oil. Allow it a minute to heat up, then add cumin seeds and the bay leaf. When the cumin seeds turn brown, add the rice and lentils (moong dal) along with the 6 cups of water, salt and turmeric.

3. Secure the lid, close the pressure valve and cook for 20 minutes at high pressure.

4. Naturally release pressure for 20 minutes. Open the valve to release any remaining pressure.

5. Serve each bowl with a spoonful of ghee and a pinch of salt.

MASALA
DAL

This is one of my go-to recipes to make on a rainy day because it's both comforting and flavorful. I love the combination of chana dal and toor dal, but you can make this recipe with a different type of split lentil if you want to change things up.

Serves 3-4

½ cup split chickpeas (chana dal),
soaked for 1-2 hours

½ cup split pigeon peas (toor dal),
soaked for 1-2 hours

4 tablespoons oil of choice

1 teaspoon cumin seeds

1 teaspoon black mustard seeds

1 onion, chopped

1 Serrano pepper
or green chili, minced

1 teaspoon minced garlic

1 teaspoon minced ginger

2 tomatoes, chopped

SPICES

1 ¼ teaspoon salt

½ teaspoon coriander powder

½ teaspoon paprika

½ teaspoon turmeric

¼ black pepper

¼ teaspoon cayenne

2 ½ cups water

¼ teaspoon garam masala

1.   Soak the lentils in cold water for 1-2 hours. Drain, rinse and set aside.

2.   Press the sauté button, add the oil and allow it to heat up for a minute. Add the cumin seeds and mustard seeds to the pot. Once the cumin seeds brown and the mustard seeds begin to pop, add the onion and Serrano pepper. Stir-fry for 6-7 minutes or until the onions begin to brown.

3.   Add the garlic and ginger and stir-fry for 30 seconds.

4.   Add the tomatoes and cook for 8-10 minutes, or until they completely break down.

5.   Add all of the spices except for the garam masala, stir, then add the lentils and water and mix well.

6.   Secure the lid, close the pressure valve and cook for 7 minutes at high pressure.

7.   Naturally release pressure.

8.   Stir in the garam masala and serve.

YELLOW LENTILS
WITH SPINACH

PALAK MOONG DAL

Serves 4-5

These creamy spiced lentils are so easy to make and they're delicious. This dish requires little effort and so it's my go-to dal on days when I'm too tired to cook. It has kept us from ordering take out on several occasions. I typically serve this dal served with basmati rice and a big salad.

1 cup small yellow lentils
(moong dal), soaked for 15 minutes

2 tablespoons oil of choice

1 teaspoon cumin seeds

2 teaspoons minced garlic

1 teaspoon minced ginger

½ Serrano pepper
or green chili, minced

SPICES

1 ½ teaspoons salt,
adjust to taste

1 teaspoon coriander powder

½ teaspoon turmeric

Pinch of cayenne, optional

4 cups water

ADD LATER

½ teaspoon garam masala

2 cups baby spinach

Cilantro, garnish

Ghee, for serving

1. Soak the small yellow lentils (moong dal) in cold water for 15 minutes. Drain, rinse and set aside.

2. Press the sauté button. Add the oil, and allow it to heat up for a minute. Add the cumin seeds to the pot. Once they turn brown, add the garlic, ginger and Serrano pepper. Stir-fry for 30 seconds, then add the spices. Give everything a quick stir, then add the water and lentils.

3. Secure the lid, close the pressure valve and cook for 15 minutes at high pressure.

4. Naturally release pressure for 10 minutes. Open the valve to release any remaining pressure.

5. Stir in the garam masala and the spinach leaves. Once the leaves begin to wilt, garnish with cilantro and serve with a spoonful of ghee on top.

KIDNEY BEAN
CURRY

RAJMA

Serves 4

Growing up with two Punjabi parents, this dish was in our regular dinner rotation. I used to dislike rajma as a kid but once I got to college, I really missed eating it. I still remember the surprise on my mom's face when I asked her if she'd make it for me. Now, it's one of my favorite dishes and whenever I do eat it, I relish every bite. These melt-in-your-mouth kidney beans are coated in a thick masala gravy and they're loaded with flavor. This dish is typically served with rice.

2 cups dried kidney beans, soaked overnight

1 onion, roughly chopped

½ Serrano pepper or green chili

3 tablespoons oil of choice

1 teaspoon cumin seeds

1 bay leaf

2 teaspoons minced garlic

2 teaspoons minced ginger

SPICES

2 ½ teaspoons salt

1 teaspoon coriander powder

1 teaspoon garam masala

1 teaspoon paprika

½ teaspoon black pepper

½ teaspoon turmeric

Pinch of cayenne, optional

2 cups fresh tomato puree (approx. 1 pound tomatoes)

2 cups water

Cilantro, garnish

1. Soak the kidney beans in cold water overnight. Drain, rinse and set aside.

2. Add the onion and Serrano pepper to a food processer and blend until smooth. Set aside.

3. Press the sauté button. Add the oil and allow it to heat up for a minute. Add the cumin seeds and once they become brown, add the blended onion and Serrano pepper to the pot and stir-fry for 8-10 minutes, or until the onion mixture begins to brown.

4. Add the bay leaf, garlic, ginger, and spices and stir quickly, then add the pureed tomatoes and cook for 5 minutes, stirring occasionally.

5. Add the kidney beans and water.

6. Secure the lid, close the pressure valve and cook for 30 minutes at high pressure.

7. Naturally release pressure.

8. Garnish with cilantro and serve with rice.

BROWN CHICKPEA **CURRY**

KALA CHANA

Serves 2-3

These brown chickpeas have a "meaty" quality to them. While they do soften after cooking, they don't absorb much liquid or break down the way other legumes or lentils do. Because of this reason, I only use a little water in this recipe. I enjoy eating this curry over basmati rice.

1 cup brown chickpeas (kala chana), soaked overnight

2 tablespoons oil of choice

1 bay leaf

½ teaspoon cumin seeds

1 onion, diced

2 teaspoons minced garlic

1 teaspoons minced ginger

SPICES

1 teaspoon salt, adjust to taste

½ teaspoon dried mango powder (amchur)

½ teaspoon garam masala

¼ teaspoon black pepper

¼ teaspoon cayenne

¼ teaspoon coriander powder

¼ teaspoon paprika

¼ teaspoon turmeric

½ cup canned tomato sauce

1 cup water

Cilantro, garnish

1. Soak the brown chickpeas in cold water overnight. Drain, rinse and set aside.

2. Press the sauté button, add the oil and allow it to heat up for a minute. Once the oil is hot, add the bay leaf and cumin seeds to the pot. Once the cumin seeds turn brown, add the onions and stir-fry for about 10 minutes, or until the onions begin to brown.

3. Add the garlic, ginger and spices and stir-fry for 30 seconds. Add the tomato sauce, brown chickpeas, water and mix well.

4. Secure the lid, close the pressure valve and cook for 45 minutes at high pressure.

5. Naturally release pressure.

6. If you prefer a thicker curry, you can reduce the liquid by pressing the sauté button once the dish is done.

7. Garnish with cilantro and serve.

LENTILS IN
COCONUT
CURRY

KERALA PARIPPU

Serves 2-3

This rich and creamy Kerala-style parippu (another word for "dal") is one of the main dishes served during Onam, a harvest festival celebrated by people of all religions in the state of Kerala. It's a simple and flavorful recipe made with coconut milk. Serve this dal with ghee drizzled on top!

1 cup split pigeon peas (toor dal), soaked for 2 hours

1 tablespoon coconut oil

½ teaspoon black mustard seeds

30 curry leaves

1 ½ cups water

1 (13.5 ounce) can of full-fat coconut milk

½ - 1 Serrano pepper or green chili, minced

1 ½ teaspoons salt

½ teaspoon ground cumin

¼ teaspoon turmeric

Ghee, for serving

1. Soak the split pigeon peas (toor dal) in cold water for 2 hours. Drain, rinse and set aside.

2. Press the sauté button, add the coconut oil to the pot. Once the coconut oil melts, add mustard seeds and curry leaves to the pot. When the mustard seeds begin to pop, add the remaining ingredients to the pot.

3. Secure the lid, close the pressure valve and cook for 10 minutes at high pressure.

4. Naturally release pressure.

5. Drizzle ghee on top prior to serving if desired.

BLACK EYED PEA **CURRY**

PUNJABI LOBIA MASALA

Serves 2-3

This popular Punjabi dish, also known as lobia masala, is made with buttery black eyed peas. This is a recipe that's almost always served on New Year's Day in our house because it's thought to bring good luck. Don't wait until then to make this though!

1 cup dried black eyed peas, soaked for 1-2 hours

2 tablespoons oil of choice

½ teaspoon cumin seeds

1 onion, diced

1 bay leaf

3 teaspoons minced garlic

1 teaspoon minced ginger

SPICES

1 teaspoon garam masala

1 teaspoon salt, adjust to taste

1 teaspoon turmeric

¼ teaspoon black pepper

⅛ - ¼ teaspoon cayenne, to taste

1 tomato, diced

2 cups water

Cilantro leaves, garnish

1. Soak the dried black eyed peas in cold water for 1-2 hours. Drain, rinse and set aside.

2. Press the sauté button, add the oil and allow it to heat up for a minute. Add the cumin seeds and once they begin to turn brown, add the onion and bay leaf. Stir-fry for 6-7 minutes, or until the onions begin to turn brown.

3. Add the garlic, ginger and spices, stir, then add the diced tomatoes. Cook for 2-3 minutes, or until the tomatoes break down.

4. Add the drained black eyed peas to the pot along with the 2 cups of water and mix well.

5. Secure the lid, close the pressure valve and cook for 20 minutes at high pressure.

6. Naturally release pressure.

7. Garnish with cilantro if desired.

SPICED BROWN
CHICKPEAS

SUKHE KALA CHANA MASALA

Serves 2-3

These masala-coated brown chickpeas are considered a "dry curry" and are often paired with Indian flatbread. I personally love eating them as a snack alongside a cup of chai.

2 cups dried brown chickpeas (kala chana), soaked overnight

2 tablespoons oil of choice

½ teaspoon cumin seeds

½ teaspoon black mustard seeds

SPICES

1 black cardamom

1 teaspoon salt

½ teaspoon coriander powder

½ teaspoon dried mango powder (amchur)

½ teaspoon garam masala

½ teaspoon turmeric

¼ teaspoon black pepper

¼ teaspoon black salt (kala namak)

¼ teaspoon paprika

¼ teaspoon roasted cumin powder (pg 8)

⅛ - ¼ teaspoon cayenne, optional

1 cup water

Cilantro, garnish

1.   Soak the brown chickpeas in cold water overnight. Drain, rinse and set aside.

2.   Press the sauté button, add the oil and allow it to heat up for a minute. Add the cumin seeds and mustard seeds. Once the cumin seeds become brown and the mustard seeds begin to pop, add the brown chickpeas and all of the spices. Mix well, then add the water.

3.   Secure the lid, close the pressure valve and cook for 30 minutes at high pressure.

4.   Naturally release pressure.

5.   Press the sauté button to boil off any remaining water in the pot.

6.   Garnish with cilantro.

SPICED BUTTERY
LENTILS

DAL MAKHANI

Serves 2-3

Dal Makhani is one of the most popular lentil dishes in Indian cuisine and is on the menu at almost every Indian restaurant. I have been eating these buttery lentils for as long as I can remember. My favorite meal as a kid was made up of this dal, yogurt and spicy achar (pickle). This is my mom's recipe and it's definitely restaurant-quality, if not better. It's also one of the first Indian recipes that I learned how to make. Top these lentils with as much ghee as you want - the more ghee, the merrier!

1 cup whole and split lentils
(any combination of: whole black lentils, whole mung beans, red lentils, red kidney beans, etc), soaked overnight

2 tablespoons oil of choice

1 tablespoon cumin seeds

1 onion, chopped

1 bay leaf

3 teaspoons minced garlic

1 ½ teaspoons minced ginger

SPICES

1 teaspoon garam masala

1 teaspoon salt, adjust to taste

1 teaspoon turmeric

½ teaspoon black pepper

½ - 1 teaspoon cayenne

2 tomatoes, chopped

3 cups water

2 tablespoons ghee

Cilantro leaves, garnish

1. Soak the lentils in cold water overnight. Drain, rinse and set aside.

2. Press the sauté button, add the oil and allow it to heat up for a minute. Add the cumin seeds and once they start to brown, add the onion and bay leaf. Stir-fry for 6-7 minutes or until the onions begin to brown.

3. Add the garlic, ginger, spices and stir, then add the tomatoes. Cook for 5 minutes, or until the tomatoes break down.

4. Add the lentils to the pot along with 3 cups of water and mix well.

5. Secure the lid, close the pressure valve and cook for 30 minutes at high pressure.

6. Naturally release pressure.

7. Stir in the ghee and garnish with cilantro if desired.

LENTILS WITH FRESH DILL LEAVES

This is the perfect summer-time dal! Fresh dill leaves add a tangy, refreshing flavor to this lentil soup. For a twist on this recipe, try using fresh fenugreek (methi) leaves if you can find them at your local Indian grocery store.

Serves 2-3

½ cup split red lentils (masoor dal), soaked for 1-2 hours

½ cup split pigeon peas (toor dal), soaked for 1-2 hours

2 tablespoons oil of choice

½ teaspoon cumin seeds

½ teaspoon black mustard seeds

1 onion, diced

1 teaspoon minced garlic

1 teaspoon minced ginger

2 tomatoes, diced

SPICES

1 teaspoon coriander powder

1 teaspoon salt

½ teaspoon garam masala

½ teaspoon turmeric

¼ teaspoon black pepper

¼ teaspoon cayenne

2 ½ cups water

¼ cup chopped dill

1. Soak the lentils in cold water for 1-2 hours. Drain, rinse and set aside.

2. Press the sauté button, add the oil and allow it to heat up for a minute. Add the cumin seeds and mustard seeds to the pot. Once the cumin seeds brown and the mustard seeds begin to pop, add the onion. Stir-fry for 4-5 minutes or until the onions begin to soften.

3. Add the garlic and ginger and stir-fry for 30 seconds.

4. Add the tomatoes and spices. Stir-fry for 4-5 minutes, or until the tomatoes soften.

5. Add the lentils and water and give everything a good mix.

6. Secure the lid, close the pressure valve and cook for 10 minutes at high pressure.

7. Naturally release pressure.

8. Stir in the dill leaves and serve.

SPICED
CHICKPEA
CURRY

PUNJABI CHOLE/
CHANA MASALA

Serves 4-5

It usually takes several hours to prepare authentic Punjabi chole, but with this recipe, you can have delicious masala coated chickpeas on your plate in no time. The spices are key to making this curry, especially the dried mango powder (amchur) which adds tanginess and the roasted cumin powder which adds depth and aroma to the dish.

2 cups dried chickpeas,
  soaked overnight

2 tablespoons oil of choice

1 onion, finely chopped

1 bay leaf

2 teaspoons minced garlic

2 teaspoons minced ginger

2 tomatoes, chopped

SPICES

2 teaspoons coriander powder

2 teaspoons dried mango powder (amchur)

2 teaspoons roasted cumin powder (pg 8)

2 teaspoons salt

1 teaspoon garam masala

1 teaspoon paprika

1 teaspoon turmeric

½ teaspoon black pepper

¼ - ½ teaspoon cayenne

1 black cardamom

2 cups water

Cilantro leaves and red onion, garnish

1. Soak the chickpeas in cold water overnight. Drain, rinse and set aside.

2. Press the sauté button. Add the oil and allow it to heat it up for a minute. Add the onion and bay leaf and stir-fry for 6-7 minutes, or until the onion begins to brown.

3. Add the garlic, ginger, stir, then add the chopped tomatoes and cook for 5-7 minutes, or until they break down.

4. Add the spices, stir, then add the chickpeas and water.

5. Secure the lid, close the pressure valve and cook for 35 minutes at high pressure.

6. Naturally release pressure.

7. Discard the black cardamom and the bay leaf, garnish with red onion and chopped cilantro.

VEGETABLES

PUNJABI
POTATO & GREEN BEANS

Serves 2-3

This popular Punjabi potato and green bean stir-fry is a dry dish. I typically pair it with a saucy curry like butter chicken and some Indian flatbread or rice to make a complete meal.

2 tablespoons oil of choice

½ teaspoon cumin seeds

½ teaspoon black mustard seeds

1 onion, diced

1 ½ teaspoons minced garlic

1 ½ teaspoons minced ginger

1 tomato, chopped

1 pound green beans, chopped

2 medium potatoes
(approx. 1 pound),
chopped into 1-inch cubes

SPICES

1 teaspoon coriander powder

1 teaspoon paprika

1 teaspoon salt

1 teaspoon turmeric

½ teaspoon black pepper

¼ teaspoon cayenne,
adjust to taste

¼ cup water

Cilantro, garnish

1. Press the sauté button, add the oil and allow it to heat up for a minute. Add the cumin seeds and mustard seeds. Once the cumin seeds begin to brown and the mustard seeds begin to pop, add the onion. Stir-fry the onion for 6-7 minutes, or until it begins to brown.

2. Add the garlic and the ginger and give everything a good stir. Then add the tomato and stir-fry for 4-5 minutes, or until it begins to break down.

3. Add the green beans and potatoes then sprinkle the spices on top. Give everything a good mix then add the ¼ cup water.

4. Secure the lid, close the pressure valve and cook for 4 minutes at high pressure.

5. Open the valve to quick release any remaining pressure.

6. Garnish with cilantro.

POTATO & EGGPLANT

IN PICKLING SPICES

ACHARI ALOO BAINGAN

Serves 4

This Punjabi dish is made by cooking baby eggplants and potatoes in a blend of Indian spices typically used to make pickles (achar). It's flavorful, spicy and tangy. This dish is often eaten with Indian bread, but you can also eat it over rice with some dahi on the side (my preference). If possible, make this a day in advance as it tastes even better the next day!

8 small eggplants (approx. 1 pound)

2 tablespoons mustard oil
   or oil of choice

1 onion, diced

3 teaspoons minced garlic

2 teaspoon minced ginger

SPICES

2 teaspoons dried mango powder (amchur)

2 teaspoons fennel powder

1 teaspoon coriander powder

1 teaspoon garam masala

1 teaspoon paprika

1 teaspoon roasted cumin powder (pg 8)

1 teaspoon salt

1 teaspoon turmeric

½ teaspoon fenugreek seed powder

¼ teaspoon black pepper

¼ teaspoon carom seeds (ajwain)

¼ teaspoon nigella seeds (kalonji)

¼ - ½ teaspoon cayenne

2 medium potatoes (approx. 1 pound),
   chopped into 1-inch pieces

½ cup water

Cilantro, garnish

1.   Using a knife, make two deep slits forming an X shape at the bottom of the eggplants, making sure to keep the stem intact. Set aside.

2.   Press the sauté button then add the oil and allow it a minute to heat up. Once the oil is hot, add the onions to the pot. Stir-fry for 6-7 minutes, or until the onions begin to brown.

3.   Add the garlic, ginger, spices and stir, then add the potatoes and mix well.

4.   Add the eggplants and the water and mix well.

5.   Secure lid, close the pressure valve and cook for 4 minutes at high pressure.

6.   Open the valve to quick release any remaining pressure.

7.   Garnish with cilantro and serve.

TANGY
TOMATO & FRESH
CORN SOUP

This tomato and fresh corn soup is a perfect light meal to prepare during the spring and summer months! The yogurt adds a refreshing bright and tangy flavor to the soup. If you can't get your hands on fresh corn, then frozen corn will work too but the kernels won't be as crisp.

Serves 2

2 tablespoons oil of choice

½ teaspoon black mustard seeds

2 teaspoons minced garlic

1 teaspoon minced ginger

SPICES

½ teaspoon coriander powder

½ teaspoon paprika

½ teaspoon salt

¼ teaspoon black pepper

¼ teaspoon cayenne

¼ teaspoon roasted cumin powder (pg 8)

¼ teaspoon turmeric

1 cup canned tomato sauce

1 cup yogurt

¾ cup water

3 ears fresh corn on the cob, dehusked

1 teaspoon dried fenugreek leaves
   (kasoori methi), garnish

1.   Press the sauté button, then add the oil and allow it a minute to heat up. Add the mustard seeds and once they begin to pop, add the garlic, ginger, spices and stir, then add the tomato sauce, yogurt and water. Mix well.

2.   Place a steamer rack on top of the sauce, then place the corn on the cobs on top of the rack.

3.   Secure the lid, close the pressure valve and cook for 3 minutes at high pressure.

4.   Open the valve to quick release any remaining pressure.

5.   Using tongs, remove the corn on the cobs and once cool to touch, cut the kernels off the cob. Place the freshly cut corn pieces back into the pot along with the dried fenugreek leaves. Mix well and serve.

POTATOES &
CAULIFLOWER

ALOO GOBI

Serves 4

Aloo Gobi translates to "Potato Cauliflower." This is a very flavorful dish mainly because these two vegetables are known for their ability soak up flavor. Some prefer the cauliflower in this dish to be soft, but I prefer mine to have a bit of crunch. Adapt this recipe to your preference: use small cauliflower florets if you like soft cauliflower or keep the pieces a little larger for extra crunch.

3 tablespoons oil of choice

1 teaspoon cumin seeds

½ teaspoon black mustard seeds

1 onion, diced

½ - 1 Serrano pepper or green chili, minced

2 teaspoons minced garlic

2 teaspoons minced ginger

2 medium potatoes (approx. 1 pound),
   cut into 1-inch pieces

¼ cup water

1 cauliflower,
   cut into florets

SPICES

1 teaspoon paprika

1 teaspoon salt

1 teaspoon turmeric

½ teaspoon garam masala

¼ teaspoon cayenne,
   adjust to taste

Cilantro, garnish

1.   Press the sauté button, add the oil and allow it to heat up for a minute. Add the cumin and mustard seeds. Once the cumin seeds brown and the mustard seeds pop, add the onion and Serrano pepper. Stir-fry for 6-7 minutes, or until the onions begin to brown.

2.   Add the garlic, ginger, potatoes and and stir-fry for 30 seconds. Pour ¼ cup water into the pot, secure the lid, close the pressure valve and cook for 3 minutes at high pressure.

3.   Open the valve to quick release any remaining pressure.

4.   Remove the lid, stir the potatoes, then add the cauliflower florets and sprinkle the spices on top of the florets. Secure the lid, close the pressure valve and cook for 1 minute on high pressure. Quick release remaining pressure.

5.   Remove the lid, mix well, garnish with cilantro and serve.

VEGETABLE
KORMA

This vegetable korma is a popular Mughlai dish, a cuisine that was developed in royal Indian kitchens during the Mughal Empire. Mughlai dishes like this one are known for having creamy and rich sauces made with dried fruits, nuts and cream. This vegetable packed korma is a mild, fragrant dish that is perfect for special occasions.

Serves 4-5

ONION TOMATO SAUCE

1 onion, roughly chopped
4 cloves garlic, roughly chopped
2-inch ginger, roughly chopped
1 tomato, chopped
½ Serrano pepper or green chili

CASHEW SAUCE

1 cup water
½ cup cashews
¼ cup heavy cream
   or full-fat coconut milk

3 tablespoons ghee

¼ cup cashews

¼ cup golden raisins

½ teaspoon cumin seeds

SPICES

2 teaspoons paprika
1 teaspoon salt
1 teaspoon coriander powder
½ teaspoon turmeric powder
½ teaspoon garam masala
¼ teaspoon cayenne, adjust to taste
¼ teaspoon ground cardamom

2 cups chopped potato
   (chopped into 1-inch cubes)

1 cup water
5 cups chopped vegetables
   (peas, carrots, green beans,
   bell pepper, broccoli)

½ teaspoon dried fenugreek leaves
   (kasoori methi)

Cilantro, garnish

1. To prepare the onion tomato sauce, add the onion, garlic, ginger, tomato and Serrano pepper to a blender or food processor and puree until smooth. Set this aside.

2. Prepare the cashew sauce by blending 1 cup water, ½ cup cashews and heavy cream until smooth. Set aside.

3. Press the sauté button, add ghee, ¼ cup cashews and golden raisins to the pot. Stir-fry until the cashews turn golden. Remove the cashews and raisins from the pot and set aside.

4. Add cumin seeds to the pot. Once they begin to brown, add the onion and tomato mixture and stir-fry for 7-8 minutes, or until the onion and tomato mixture has thickened. Add all of the remaining spices along with the potatoes and mix well.

5. Add 1 cup water, secure lid, close the pressure valve and cook for 5 minutes at high pressure.

6. Open the valve to quick release any remaining pressure.

7. Add the remaining chopped vegetables. Secure the lid and cook for an additional 2 minutes at high pressure.

8. Open the valve to quick release any remaining pressure.

9. Stir in the cashew sauce and fenugreek leaves.

10. Garnish with cilantro and ghee-coated cashews and raisins.

SPICED
BUTTERY
GREENS

SAAG

Serves 5-6

I like to describe saag as the Indian version of creamed spinach, only the creaminess comes from the ghee. Saag translates to "pureed greens" so you can essentially use any green vegetable to make saag. To make authentic Punjabi saag, you will want to use a combination of mustard greens and spinach. This is the version of saag that I grew up eating and it's the one that I prefer, but if you can't find mustard greens, don't worry, spinach will work just fine too. An all spinach saag will have a thinner consistency though. Once the saag is done, you can add cooked meat or paneer to the dish if you want. Just make sure to always top your bowl with extra ghee!

2 tablespoons ghee

2 onions, diced

4 teaspoons minced garlic

2 teaspoons minced ginger

SPICES

2 teaspoons salt

1 teaspoon coriander powder

1 teaspoon garam masala

1 teaspoon ground cumin

½ teaspoon black pepper

½ teaspoon cayenne,
   adjust to taste

½ teaspoon turmeric

1 pound spinach, rinsed

1 pound mustard leaves, rinsed

Pinch of dried fenugreek leaves
   (kasoori methi)

Ghee or butter, for serving

1.   Press the sauté button and add the ghee. Once it melts, add the onion, garlic, ginger and spices to the pot and stir-fry for 2-3 minutes.

2.   Add the spinach, stirring until it wilts and there's enough room to add the mustard greens.

3.   Secure the lid, close the pressure valve and cook for 15 minutes at high pressure.

4.   Naturally release pressure.

5.   Remove the lid and use an immersion blender to puree the contents of the pot (or pour the contents into a blender and then add the blended mixture back into the pot).

6.   Stir in the dried fenugreek leaves.

7.   Serve with ghee.

POTATO & PEA
CURRY

ALOO MATAR

Serves 2-3

This popular Punjabi curry is a simple and comforting dish. I almost always have potatoes in my pantry and a bag of frozen peas in the freezer and so even when the fridge is empty, I can still create this delicious curry. Potatoes and peas are humble ingredients, but when you serve them in a fragrant spiced tomato sauce, they really shine.

2 tablespoons oil of choice

1 teaspoon cumin seeds

1 onion, diced

1 Serrano pepper or green chili, minced

2 teaspoons minced garlic

1 teaspoon minced ginger

1 cup fresh tomato puree
 (approx. ½ pound tomatoes)

SPICES

1 teaspoon salt

½ teaspoon coriander powder

½ teaspoon garam masala

½ teaspoon paprika

½ teaspoon turmeric

¼ teaspoon black pepper

⅛ teaspoon cayenne, optional

2 medium potatoes
 (approx. 1 pound), chopped

1 ½ cups water

2 cups fresh or frozen peas

1. Press the sauté button, add the oil and allow it to heat up for a minute. Add the cumin seeds, and once they brown, add the onion and Serrano pepper. Stir-fry for 6-7 minutes, or until the onions begin to brown.

2. Add the garlic and ginger and give everything a quick stir. Add the pureed tomatoes and spices to the pot. Cook the tomatoes for 5 minutes, stirring occasionally.

3. Add the potatoes and mix well, then add the water and peas to the pot.

4. Secure the lid, close the pressure valve and cook for 5 minutes at high pressure.

5. Open the valve to quick release any remaining pressure.

MASHED SPICED
EGGPLANT

BAINGAN BHARTA

Serves 2-3

This is my favorite way to eat eggplant. I know mashed eggplant may not sound very appealing, but trust me this dish tastes way better than it sounds. Baingan bharta is typically made by first cooking eggplants on a stove or a grill to give it a smoky flavor, but I've simplified the recipe to make it all in one pot and I find that it tastes about the same. And truthfully, the ease of making this dish means that I make and enjoy it a lot more often.

2 large eggplants

4 tablespoons oil of choice

1 teaspoon cumin seeds

1 onion, diced

5 teaspoons minced garlic

1 teaspoon minced ginger

SPICES

2 teaspoons coriander powder

2 teaspoons salt

1 teaspoon garam masala

½ teaspoon black pepper

½ teaspoon cayenne

½ teaspoon paprika

½ teaspoon turmeric

2 tomatoes, diced

¼ cup water

Cilantro, garnish

1. Peel the eggplants and chop them into chunks. Set aside.

2. Press the sauté button, add the oil and allow it to heat up for a minute. Add the cumin seeds and once they turn brown, add the onion and stir-fry for 6-7 minutes, or until they start to brown.

3. Add garlic, ginger, spices, stir-fry for 30 seconds, then add tomatoes. Cook for 4-5 minutes, or until the tomatoes begin to break down.

4. Add the eggplant and water, mix well.

5. Secure the lid, close the pressure valve and cook for 7 minutes at high pressure.

6. Open the valve to quick release any remaining pressure.

7. Open the lid and mash the eggplant. Press sauté and cook for 2-3 minutes to boil off any extra liquid if desired.

8. Garnish with cilantro and serve.

MUSHROOMS
IN AN
ONION GRAVY

MUSHROOM DO PYAZA

Serves 2-3

Do Pyaza means "two onions," and so if you see these words in the name of a dish, then you can expect there to be plenty of onions in the recipe. Not only does this recipe call for lots of onions, it also calls for preparing the onions two different ways: caramelizing the onions and stir-frying them. If you love mushrooms and onions, you will love this dish!

2 tablespoons oil of choice

2 onions, diced

2 teaspoons minced garlic

2 teaspoons minced ginger

2 tomatoes, diced

1 pound mushrooms, sliced

SPICES

5 whole cloves

1 ¼ teaspoons salt

1 ¼ teaspoons turmeric

½ teaspoon coriander powder

½ teaspoon paprika

½ teaspoon roasted cumin powder (pg 8)

¼ teaspoon black pepper

⅛ - ¼ teaspoon cayenne

⅛ teaspoon ground cardamom

2 tablespoons water

ADD LATER

1 bell pepper,
   cut into large pieces

1 onion,
   cut into large pieces

1.   Press the sauté button, add the oil and allow it to heat up for a minute.

2.   Add the diced onions and stir-fry for 8-10 minutes, or until they begin to brown.

3.   Add the garlic and ginger, stir, then add the tomatoes and cook for 4-5 minutes, or until they break down.

4.   Add the mushrooms and spices and mix well.

5.   Add the water, mix well, then secure the lid, close the pressure valve and cook for 5 minutes at high pressure.

6.   Open the valve to quick release any remaining pressure.

7.   Add the bell pepper and onion to the pot, press the sauté button, and stir-fry for 5 minutes, or until the onion and bell pepper have softened.

TARO ROOT
DELIGHT

ARBI

Serves 3-4

Taro root, also known as "arbi," is one of my favorite vegetables, probably because it reminds me so much of a potato. In this recipe, Taro root "coins" are cooked in a delicious, spiced gravy. I couldn't figure out what to call this recipe, so my husband came up with the name "Taro Root Delight." This dish really is delightful! It's kind of like an Indian version of scalloped potatoes.

1 pound taro root,
  peeled and sliced into ¼ inch thick coins

3 tablespoons oil of choice

1 onion, diced

1 bay leaf

1 teaspoon minced garlic

½ teaspoon minced ginger

SPICES

½ teaspoon dried mango powder (amchur)

½ teaspoon salt

¼ teaspoon black salt (kala namak)

¼ teaspoon carom seeds (ajwain)

¼ teaspoon coriander powder

¼ teaspoon garam masala

¼ teaspoon roasted cumin powder (pg 8)

¼ teaspoon turmeric

⅛ teaspoon black pepper

⅛ teaspoon cayenne

¾ cup water

Cilantro, garnish

1. Rinse the peeled taro roots and place them on a paper towel-lined plate to dry. This will help make them less slippery so that you can slice them safely.

2. Press the sauté button, add the oil and allow it a minute to warm up. Add the onion and bay leaf and stir-fry for 6-7 minutes, or until the onion begins to brown.

3. Add the garlic, ginger, spices, taro root and stir, then add the water and mix well.

4. Secure the lid, close the pressure valve and cook for 5 minutes at high pressure.

5. Naturally release pressure.

6. Discard the bay leaf, garnish with chopped cilantro and serve.

POTATOES IN A CREAMY
CASHEW
TOMATO SAUCE

DUM ALOO

Serves 3-4

When I first made dum aloo for the family, my husband told me he didn't think the potatoes were very "dumb." He was joking of course (I'm thankful to be married to a guy with my cheesy sense of humor). "Dum" refers to a type of cooking method where food is cooked slowly over low heat in a sealed pot, which helps retain steam which in turn keeps the dish moist. These baby potatoes are cooked over high heat in a short amount of time, so it's true they aren't "dum" but the flavor of dum aloo is the same.

11-12 baby potatoes
  (approx. 1½ pound), peeled

ONION TOMATO SAUCE

1 onion, roughly chopped

2 garlic cloves, roughly chopped

1-inch ginger, roughly chopped

2 tomatoes, roughly chopped

CREAMY CASHEW SAUCE

⅓ cup cashews

½ cup water

1 tablespoon oil of choice

SPICES

2 teaspoons paprika

1 teaspoon garam masala

1 teaspoon salt

½ teaspoon turmeric

¼ teaspoon cayenne

½ cup water

1 teaspoon dried fenugreek leaves
  (kasoori methi)

2 tablespoons heavy cream or yogurt or
  coconut milk, optional

1. Prick the potatoes in several places with a fork.

2. Add the onion, garlic, ginger and tomatoes to a blender or food processor and puree until smooth. Set aside.

3. To make the creamy cashew sauce, add the cashews and ½ cup water to the blender and puree until smooth. Set aside.

4. Press the sauté button and add oil and the blended onion and tomato mixture. Stir-fry for 8-10 minutes until the mixture has thickened.

5. Add the spices and the potatoes and mix well, then add ½ cup water to the pot.

6. Secure the lid, close the pressure valve and cook for 8 minutes at high pressure.

7. Open the valve to quick release any remaining pressure.

8. Stir in the cashew sauce, fenugreek leaves and heavy cream if using.

GREEN BEAN
STIR-FRY

GREEN BEAN THORAN

Serves 2-3

Like most recipes for "thoran" (stir-fry), this green bean dish is made with a few spices, grated coconut and curry leaves. This is a common side dish served in Keralite homes and can be made with all sorts of vegetables. My husband has been eating thoran all his life and has tried just about every type of thoran one can have - and green bean thoran is his favorite (beet thoran is my favorite - see page 46 for that recipe).

1 pound green beans, chopped

1 tablespoon coconut oil

½ teaspoon black mustard seeds

½ onion, finely diced

2 teaspoons minced garlic

¼ Serrano pepper or green chili, minced, adjust to taste

15 curry leaves

½ cup grated coconut*

½ teaspoon turmeric

½ teaspoon salt

¼ cup water

1. Chop the green beans into small pieces and set aside.

2. Press the sauté button then add the coconut oil. Once it melts, add the mustard seeds. When the mustard seeds begin to pop, add the onion, garlic, Serrano pepper and curry leaves. Stir-fry for 1-2 minutes, then add the green beans, coconut, turmeric and salt.

3. Give everything a quick stir, then pour the water into the pot.

4. Secure the lid, close the pressure valve and cook for 1 minute at high pressure.

5. Open the valve to quick release any remaining pressure.

6. Stir everything together until well combined. If there's any water remaining in the pot, press sauté to boil it off.

*Find frozen unsweetened grated coconut at your local Indian grocery store.

SPICED
TURNIPS

SHALGAM KI SABZI

Serves 3-4

This is a North Indian recipe that's often served during the fall and winter. Like cauliflower and potatoes, turnips also tend to absorb flavor really well. Some prefer to puree the turnips after cooking them and eat this as a mashed dish (bhartha), but I personally prefer the soft texture of cooked turnips. Serve this sabzi (cooked vegetable) with Indian flatbread.

2 tablespoons ghee

1 teaspoon cumin seeds

1 teaspoon black mustard seeds

1 bay leaf

1 onion, diced

1 teaspoon garlic

1 teaspoon ginger

½ Serrano pepper or green chili, minced

SPICES

1 teaspoon coriander powder

1 teaspoon dried mango powder (amchur)

1 teaspoon garam masala

1 teaspoon salt

½ teaspoon paprika

½ teaspoon turmeric

¼ teaspoon black pepper

¼ teaspoon cayenne

½ cup canned tomato sauce

1 tablespoon sugar,
 coconut sugar or jaggery

2 pounds turnips, chopped

2 tablespoons water

Cilantro, garnish

1.   Press the sauté button then add the ghee. Once the ghee melts, add cumin seeds, mustard seeds and bay leaf to the pot. When the cumin seeds brown and and the mustard seeds begin to pop, add the onions and stir-fry for 5 minutes or until the onions soften.

2.   Add the garlic, ginger, Serrano pepper and spices and stir-fry for 30 seconds. Then add the tomato sauce, sugar, turnips, water and mix well.

3.   Secure the lid, close the pressure valve and cook for 5 minutes at high pressure.

4.   Open the valve to quick release any remaining pressure.

5.   Garnish with cilantro.

BEET
STIR-FRY

BEET THORAN

Serves 2-3

It's no secret that I love beets - after all, the name of my blog is My Heart Beets. This simple beet recipe is one of my all-time favorite side dishes to make when preparing a Keralite meal. In the past, I would chop or grate raw beets (which isn't very easy to do) and then cook them but with this recipe, I first steam the beets, chop them up, then stir-fry them. It's so much easier to make which means we eat it far more often. If you decide to use small or large beets for this dish, you may need to adjust the cooking time.

5 medium beets

1 tablespoon coconut oil

1 teaspoon black mustard seeds

½ onion, finely diced

¼ Serrano pepper or green chili, adjust to taste

1 teaspoon minced garlic

20 curry leaves

½ teaspoon turmeric

½ teaspoon salt

¼ cup grated coconut*

*Find frozen unsweetened grated coconut at your local Indian grocery store.

You may need to adjust the cooking time depending on the size of the beets.

1. To prepare the beets, add 2 cups water into the steel inner pot, then place a steamer basket or the wire rack that came with your pressure cooker into the pot. Place the unpeeled beets on top of the rack, then secure the lid, close the pressure valve, press the steam button and set the time for 15 minutes at high pressure.

2. Open the valve to quick release any remaining pressure.

3. Once the the beets are cool enough to touch, remove them from the pot. The peels should easily slide off. Place the beets on a cutting board and chop them into small pieces. Set aside.

4. Dump out any water still remaining in the bottom of the pot, then press the sauté button and add the coconut oil. Once the coconut oil melts, add the mustard seeds. When the mustard seeds begin to pop, add the onion, Serrano pepper, garlic and curry leaves. Stir-fry for 3-4 minutes, or until the onions are cooked through.

5. Add the turmeric and salt, stir, then add the cooked beets and mix well. Stir in the grated coconut.

MIXED VEGETABLES IN
YOGURT SAUCE

AVIAL

Serves 3-4

I love this mixed vegetable dish because it's so easy to make and it always seems to impress guests who aren't used to eating a variety of Indian vegetables (such as green plantain, taro root or drumsticks).

1 tablespoon coconut oil

½ teaspoon black mustard seeds

30 curry leaves

4 cups assorted vegetables*,
    cut lengthwise (2-inch long pieces)

½ cup grated coconut**

⅔ cup water

1 Serrano pepper or green chili,
    slit in half but still in-tact

1 teaspoon salt, adjust to taste

½ teaspoon ground cumin

¼ teaspoon turmeric

½ cup yogurt

1. Press the sauté button then add the coconut oil. Once it melts, add the mustard seeds and curry leaves. When the mustard seeds begin to pop, add the remaining ingredients to the pot except for the yogurt.

2. Secure the lid, close the pressure valve and cook for 4 minutes at high pressure.

3. Open the valve to quick release the pressure.

4. Stir in the yogurt and serve immediately or at room temperature.

This dish is typically made with assorted vegetables such as unripe plaintan, unripe green mango, carrots, green beans, cucumber, pumpkin, taro root, potatoes. It is also often made with moringa, which is better known as drumstick. If you use drumsticks in this recipe, you are to eat the inside and then discard the fibrous exterior. You can find drumsticks as well as a variety of other Indian vegetables in the frozen aisle of any Indian grocery store.

**Find frozen unsweetened grated coconut at your local Indian grocery store.*

CABBAGE
AND PEAS

This recipe for shredded cabbage and peas is a simple side dish that calls for a handful of basic Indian spices. I recommend serving this dish alongside lentils or a meat based curry.

Serves 4-5

2 tablespoons oil of choice

1 teaspoon black mustard seeds

1 teaspoon minced ginger

1 small cabbage (approx. 28 ounces), shredded

1 cup frozen peas

SPICES

1 teaspoon coriander powder

1 teaspoon turmeric

½ teaspoon paprika

½ teaspoon salt

¼ teaspoon black pepper

¼ teaspoon cayenne, adjust to taste

1 tablespoon water

Cilantro, garnish

1. Press the sauté button, add the oil and allow it to heat up for a minute. Once it's hot, add the mustard seeds. When the mustard seeds begin to pop, add the ginger, stir, then add the cabbage and peas. Sprinkle the spices on top, add the water and give everything a good mix.

2. Secure the lid, close the pressure valve and cook for 3 minutes at high pressure.

3. Open the valve to quick release any remaining pressure.

4. Mix well, garnish with cilantro and serve

CHICKEN
& EGGS

CHICKEN
BIRYANI

Serves 4

This flavorful chicken biryani is a family-favorite. Biryani, a well-seasoned meat and rice dish, typically takes a long time to prepare and requires dirtying several dishes but this one-pot recipe is just as good as the traditional version and creates less mess! It takes just 10 minutes of prep time and can be ready-to-eat in under an hour. It's easy enough to make on a weeknight and impressive enough to serve to your guests at a dinner party.

1 cup basmati rice, soaked 15-30 minutes

3 tablespoons ghee

⅓ cup cashews, halved

2 tablespoons golden raisins

WHOLE SPICES

5 cardamom pods

4 whole cloves

2 bay leaf

½ cinnamon stick

½ teaspoon cumin seeds

½ teaspoon fennel seeds

1 onion, thinly sliced

4 teaspoons minced garlic

2 teaspoons minced ginger

1 ½ pounds skinless and boneless chicken thighs, cut into quarters

GROUND SPICES

2 teaspoons coriander powder

2 teaspoons paprika

2 teaspoons salt, adjust to taste

1 teaspoon garam masala

¼ teaspoon black pepper

¼ teaspoon cayenne, adjust to taste

¼ teaspoon ground cumin

¼ teaspoon turmeric

1 cup water

½ cup fresh cilantro leaves, chopped

½ cup fresh mint leaves, chopped

1. Soak the basmati rice in cold water for 15-30 minutes. Drain, rinse and set aside.

2. Press the sauté button. Add the ghee to the pot. When it melts, add the cashews and raisins. Stir-fry until the cashews begin to turn golden. Remove the cashews and raisins. Set aside.

3. Add the whole spices and stir. Once they begin to sizzle add the onions. Stir-fry for 6-7 minutes or until they begin to brown.

4. Add the garlic and ginger and stir-fry for 30 seconds.

5. Add the chicken and stir-fry 6-7 minutes or until the outside of the chicken is no longer pink.

6. Add the ground spices and mix to coat the chicken.

7. Dump the rice on top of the chicken (do not mix). Add water. Sprinkle half the cilantro and mint on top of the rice.

8. Secure the lid, close the pressure valve and cook for 6 minutes at high pressure.

9. Naturally release pressure for 10 minutes. Open the valve to release any remaining pressure.

10. Discard the whole spices. Sprinkle with remaining cilantro and mint and garnish with the ghee-coated cashews and raisins.

BUTTER
CHICKEN
MURGH MAKHANI

Serves 4

This is one of the most popular recipes on my blog! It truly is restaurant-quality, if not better. There's one ingredient listed below that you may not have used before: dried fenugreek leaves, also known as kasoori methi. Even though this recipe only calls for a small amount, this particular ingredient gives butter chicken it's distinct taste. I know it might take a little effort to find this ingredient, but please try! I buy dried fenugreek leaves from either Amazon or my local Indian grocery store.

2 tablespoons ghee

1 onion, diced

5 teaspoons minced garlic

1 teaspoon minced ginger

1 ½ pounds skinless and boneless
   chicken thighs, cut into quarters

SPICES

1 teaspoon coriander powder

1 teaspoon garam masala

1 teaspoon paprika

1 teaspoon salt

1 teaspoon turmeric

¼ teaspoon black pepper

¼ teaspoon cayenne, adjust to taste

¼ teaspoon ground cumin

1 (15 ounce) can tomato sauce

ADD LATER

2 green bell peppers,
   chopped in large pieces

½ cup heavy cream
   or full-fat coconut milk

Pinch of dried fenugreek leaves
   (kasoori methi)

Cilantro, garnish

1. Press the sauté button and add the ghee and onions to the pot. Stir-fry the onions for 6-7 minutes or until the onions begin to brown.

2. Add the garlic, ginger and chicken. Stir-fry the chicken for 6-7 minutes or until the outside of the chicken is no longer pink.

3. Add the spices and give everything a good mix. Stir in the tomato sauce.

4. Secure the lid, close the pressure valve and cook for 8 minutes at high pressure.

5. Open the valve to quick release any remaining pressure.

6. Press the sauté button, add the bell peppers and cook until they soften to your liking.

7. Stir in the cream and fenugreek leaves.

8. Garnish with cilantro if desired, then serve.

TANDOORI
CHICKEN WINGS

These tandoori chicken wings are so tasty and easy to make! You just steam the wings in the pressure cooker, coat them in a flavorful spiced yogurt sauce and then pop them in the oven so they develop a nice crust. You can do this with any sauce!

Serves 4

25 wings (approx 2.5 pounds)

TANDOORI WING SAUCE

1 cup yogurt

1 tablespoon lemon juice

1 tablespoon minced garlic

1 tablespoon minced ginger

1 tablespoon paprika

2 teaspoons salt

1 ½ teaspoons coriander powder

½ teaspoon cayenne, adjust to taste

½ teaspoon garam masala

¼ teaspoon ground cardamom

¼ teaspoon ground cumin

¼ teaspoon ground fennel

Pinch ground cloves

1.   Place 2 cups of water into the steel inner pot, then place a steamer basket inside. Place the wings in the steamer basket. Secure the lid, close the pressure valve and cook for 10 minutes at high pressure.

2.   Preheat the oven to 425°F. Prepare a large foil-lined pan and then place a wire rack on top of the pan. Set aside.

3.   Prepare the tandoori wing sauce by combining all of the remaining ingredients together in a large bowl. Set aside.

4.   When the wings are done, open the valve to quick release any remaining pressure. Use tongs to place the wings on a paper-towel lined plate and pat them dry.

5.   Put the wings in the large bowl with the wing sauce, then place them onto the wire rack sitting on top of the foil-lined sheet pan.

6.   Bake the wings at 425°F for 5 minutes. Then take the wings out of the oven. Using a basting brush, add more sauce onto the wings. Place the wings back into the oven for an additional 10 minutes.

KERALA
COCONUT
CHICKEN STEW

Serves 4

This lightly spiced coconut chicken stew is a dish that's often served for breakfast in Keralite homes. I love making it for Sunday brunch! As someone who grew up in a North Indian family, I find the flavor of this curry to be very different from the dishes that I grew up eating. I learned how to make this stew after watching my mother-in-law make it many times. I love the flavor of curry leaf spiced coconut milk with chicken and potatoes. I hope you love this as much as I do.

2 tablespoons coconut oil

1 red onion, thinly sliced

20-30 curry leaves

1 ½ pounds skinless and boneless chicken thighs, cut into quarters

1 teaspoon minced ginger

SPICES

1 teaspoon coriander powder

1 teaspoon meat masala (pg 8)

1 teaspoon salt

½ teaspoon black pepper

½ teaspoon turmeric

¼ teaspoon cayenne

2 medium potatoes (approx. 1 pound), peeled and cubed

2 carrots, sliced

1 (13.5 ounce) can full-fat coconut milk

1.   Press sauté, add the coconut oil and when it melts, add the onion. Stir-fry for 10-12 minutes or until they turn brown. Remove some of the onions and set them aside to use as a garnish.

2.   Add the curry leaves and the chicken. Stir-fry for 8-9 minutes, or until the chicken is no longer no longer pink and is mostly cooked through.

3.   Add the ginger and ground spices and give everything a good mix so that the chicken is coated with all of the spices.

4.   Add the potatoes and carrots, stir, then add the coconut milk.

5.   Secure the lid, close the pressure valve and cook for 4 minutes at high pressure.

6.   Naturally release pressure for 10 minutes. Open the valve to release any remaining pressure.

7.   Garnish with the browned onions and serve.

CHICKEN TIKKA
MASALA
AND RICE

Chicken tikka masala, a creamy spiced tomato chicken curry, is said to be a British invention. I decided to invent a new dish by adding rice to the curry, making it a one-pot meal.

Serves 4

1 ½ cups basmati rice,
   soaked for 15-30 minutes

3 tablespoons oil of choice

1 onion, diced

4 teaspoons minced garlic

1 teaspoons minced ginger

1 Serrano pepper or green chili, minced

1 ½ - 2 pounds skinless and boneless
   chicken thighs, cut into quarters

SPICES

2 teaspoons coriander powder

2 teaspoons paprika

2 teaspoons salt

1 teaspoon garam masala

½ teaspoon ground cumin

½ teaspoon turmeric

¼ teaspoon ground cardamom

¼ teaspoon cayenne

1 cup canned tomato sauce

¼ cup heavy cream
   or full-fat coconut milk

1 cup water

Cilantro, garnish

1. Soak the basmati rice in cold water for 15-30 minutes. Drain, rinse and set aside.

2. Press the sauté button and add the oil and onions to the pot. Stir-fry for 6-7 minutes, or until they begin to brown.

3. Add the garlic, ginger, Serrano pepper, stir, then add the chicken and stir-fry for 5-6 minutes or until the outside of the chicken is no longer pink.

4. Add the spices, give the pot a quick stir, then add the tomato sauce and heavy cream.

5. Pour 1 cup of water and the rice into the pot and mix well.

6. Secure the lid, close the pressure valve and cook for 6 minutes at high pressure.

7. Naturally release pressure for 10 minutes. Open the valve to release any remaining pressure.

8. Sprinkle with cilantro and serve.

CHICKEN
KORMA

Serves 4-5

This dish, also known as Shahi Chicken Korma, is a royal entree typically served on special occasions. A korma is a mildly spiced curry that calls for dried fruit (raisins) and nuts. For this recipe, the creaminess comes from well-blended cashews. This gives the sauce a thick, rich feel and flavor.

ONION TOMATO MIXTURE

1 onion, roughly chopped

4 garlic cloves, roughly chopped

1-inch ginger, roughly chopped

½ Serrano pepper or green chili, roughly chopped

1 tomato, roughly chopped

CREAMY CASHEW SAUCE

½ cup cashews

½ cup water

3 tablespoons ghee

¼ cup cashews

¼ cup golden raisins

½ teaspoon cumin seeds

SPICES

1 ½ teaspoons salt, adjust to taste

1 teaspoon coriander powder

1 teaspoon paprika

1 teaspoon turmeric

½ teaspoon garam masala

½ teaspoon ground cumin

¼ teaspoon cayenne

¼ teaspoon cinnamon

¼ teaspoon ground cardamom

1 ½ pounds skinless and boneless chicken thighs, cut into quarters

1 cup water

1 teaspoon dried fenugreek leaves (kasoori methi)

Cilantro, garnish

1. To make the onion tomato mixture, add the onion, garlic, ginger, Serrano pepper and tomato to a blender or food processor and puree until smooth. Set aside.

2. Prepare the cashew sauce by adding the cashews and ½ cup water to a blender and blend until smooth. Set aside.

3. Press the sauté button and add ghee, ¼ cup of cashews and golden raisins. Stir-fry until the cashews begin to turn golden. Remove the cashews and raisins and set aside to use as a garnish.

4. Add cumin seeds and once they begin to brown, add the blended onion and tomato mixture. Stir-fry for 8-10 minutes, or until the onion and tomato mixture has thickened.

5. Add the spices, stir, then add the chicken and mix well.

6. Pour 1 cup of water into the pot.

7. Secure the lid, close the pressure valve and cook for 10 minutes at high pressure.

8. Open the valve to quick release any remaining pressure.

9. Press the sauté button, add the cashew sauce and fenugreek leaves and cook for 2-3 minutes.

10. Garnish with cilantro, ghee-coated cashews and raisins.

CHICKEN CURRY
IN PICKLING SPICES
ACHARI CHICKEN CURRY

Serves 4

This chicken curry is made with spices that are typically used to make Indian pickles, also known as achar. It's a very flavorful and aromatic curry. Like many Indian dishes, this curry will taste even better the next day when you eat the leftovers.

3 tablespoons oil of choice

1 teaspoon cumin seeds

1 bay leaf

1 onion, diced

1 teaspoon minced garlic

1 teaspoon minced ginger

SPICES

1 teaspoon coriander powder

1 teaspoon fennel seeds

1 teaspoon paprika

1 teaspoon salt

1 teaspoon turmeric

½ teaspoon dried mango powder (amchur)

½ teaspoon fenugreek (methi) seeds

½ teaspoon garam masala

½ teaspoon nigella seeds (kalonji)

¼ teaspoon black pepper

¼ teaspoon cayenne

2 pounds skinless and boneless chicken thighs, cut into bite-sized pieces

1 cup fresh tomato puree (approx. ½ pound tomatoes)

½ cup water

Cilantro, garnish

1. Press the sauté button, add the oil and allow it to heat up for a minute. Add the cumin seeds and once they brown, add the bay leaf and onions. Stir-fry for 6-7 minutes, or until the onions begin to brown.

2. Add garlic, ginger, spices and stir briefly. Add the chicken and give everything a good mix so that the chicken is well coated with the spices.

3. Add the pureed tomatoes and cook for 5 minutes, stirring occasionally. Then add the water.

4. Secure the lid, close the pressure valve and cook for 5 minutes at high pressure.

5. Naturally release pressure.

6. Garnish with cilantro.

MANGO
CHICKEN

This sweet and savory chicken curry is so delicious! Most restaurants use sweetened canned mango to make this dish, but my recipe calls for fresh mango puree and that makes all the difference! The curry leaves add a nice aroma to the dish and pair perfectly with the mango and coconut milk.

Serves 4

1 onion, roughly chopped

2 garlic cloves, roughly chopped

1-inch ginger, roughly chopped

2 tablespoons oil of choice

WHOLE SPICES

½ teaspoon black mustard seeds

10-12 curry leaves

5 cardamom pods

¼ cinnamon stick

SPICES

1 ½ teaspoons salt

1 teaspoon paprika

1 teaspoon turmeric

¼ teaspoon black pepper

¼ teaspoon cayenne

1 ½ pounds skinless and boneless chicken thighs, cut into quarters

1 cup water

ADD LATER

1 cup fresh mango puree (from ripe mangoes)

½ cup full-fat canned coconut milk

1 tablespoon sugar, optional

Cilantro, garnish

1.　Add the onion, garlic, ginger, to a blender or food processor and puree until smooth. Set aside.

2.　Press sauté, add oil and allow it to heat up. Add the whole spices once they begin to sizzle, add the blended onion mixture. Stir-fry for 5-6 minutes, or until the onion mixture has thickened.

3.　Add the spices and chicken to the pot and stir-fry for 2-3 minutes, or until the chicken is well coated with spices.

4.　Pour water into the pot, secure the lid, close the pressure valve and cook for 10 minutes at high pressure.

5.　Open the valve to quick release any remaining pressure.

6.　Remove the lid, press the sauté button, add the mango puree, coconut milk and sugar into the pot. Cook for 2-3 minutes, stirring occasionally.

7.　Garnish with cilantro.

CHICKEN & POTATO **CURRY**

While there are many different types of chicken curry, I consider this recipe to be more of an everyday type of curry. Perfectly cooked chicken and tender potatoes are served in a spiced onion and tomato gravy, making this a comforting and hearty dish.

Serves 4

3 tablespoons oil of choice

½ teaspoon cumin seeds

½ teaspoon black mustard seeds

1 onion, diced

1 bay leaf

2 teaspoons minced garlic

1 teaspoon minced ginger

SPICES

1 teaspoon coriander powder

1 teaspoon paprika

1 teaspoon salt

½ teaspoon fennel powder

½ teaspoon garam masala

½ teaspoon turmeric

¼ teaspoon black pepper

¼ teaspoon carom seeds (ajwain)

¼ teaspoon cayenne

¼ teaspoon dried mango powder (amchur)

1 ½ pounds skinless and boneless chicken thighs, cut into quarters

1 cup fresh tomato puree (approx. ½ pound tomatoes)

4 small yellow or white potatoes (approx. 1 pound), cut in half

½ cup water

Cilantro, garnish

1. Press the sauté button, add the oil and allow it to heat up for a minute. Add the cumin seeds and mustard seeds and once the cumin seeds brown and the mustard seeds pop, add the onion and bay leaf. Stir-fry for 6-7 minutes, or until the onion begins to brown.

2. Add garlic, ginger, spices and stir briefly. Add the chicken and give everything a good mix so that the chicken is well coated with the spices.

3. Add the pureed tomatoes and cook for 5 minutes, stirring occasionally.

4. Add the potatoes, give everything a good stir, then pour in the water.

5. Secure the lid, close the pressure valve and cook for 5 minutes at high pressure.

6. Naturally release pressure.

7. Garnish with cilantro.

MASALA EGG
ROAST

NADAN MUTTA ROAST

Serves 3-4

The eggs in this Keralite dish are coated in a thick sauce made with ripe tomatoes and sweet caramelized onions. I love making egg curry in a pressure cooker because of how easy it is to make both the sauce and the eggs at the same time.

2 tablespoons oil of choice

½ teaspoon black mustard seeds

2 onions, thinly sliced

10-15 curry leaves

1 teaspoon minced garlic

1 teaspoon minced ginger

SPICES

3 teaspoons paprika

1 teaspoon coriander powder

1 teaspoon salt

½ teaspoon meat masala (pg 8)

¼ teaspoon turmeric

¼ teaspoon cayenne

¼ teaspoon black pepper

2 tomatoes, diced

¼ cup water

6 eggs

1. Press the sauté button, add the oil and allow it to heat up for a minute. Add the mustard seeds and once they begin to pop, add the onions and stir-fry for 8-10 minutes, or until the onions begin to brown.

2. Add the curry leaves, garlic, ginger, spices and stir, then add the tomatoes. Cook for 5 minutes, or until the tomatoes break down.

3. Add ¼ cup water, then place a steamer basket into the pot. Place the eggs on top of the steamer basket, then secure the lid, close the pressure valve and cook for 10 minutes at high pressure.

4. Open the valve to quick release any remaining pressure.

5. Remove the eggs and place them into a bowl of ice cold water for 5 minutes. Peel the eggs, and make four slits in each egg.

6. Remove the steamer basket from the pressure cooker, and place the eggs into the steel bowl with the cooked tomato sauce.

7. Press sauté and stir-fry the eggs in the sauce for about 5 minutes, or until most of the water has boiled off and the eggs are well coated in a thick sauce.

ROYAL EGG
KORMA

This silky and mildly spiced egg korma is both impressive enough to serve guests and yet easy enough to make on a weeknight. Serve this creamy curry over rice or with Indian flatbread.

Serves 3-4

ONION TOMATO SAUCE

1 onion, roughly chopped

2 cloves garlic, roughly chopped

1-inch ginger roughly chopped

1 tomato, chopped

CASHEW CREAM SAUCE

1 cup water

¼ cup heavy cream or coconut milk

¼ cup cashews

1 tablespoon white poppy seeds, soaked in 2 tablespoons water for at least 10 minutes (optional)

SPICES

1 ½ teaspoons salt, adjust to taste

1 teaspoon coriander powder

½ teaspoon garam masala

½ teaspoon paprika

½ teaspoon turmeric

¼ black pepper

¼ teaspoon cayenne, adjust to taste

¼ teaspoon ground cardamom

1 cup water

6 eggs

2 tablespoons chopped cilantro, garnish

2 tablespoons chopped mint, garnish

1. To prepare the onion tomato sauce, add the onion, garlic, ginger and tomato to a blender or food processor and puree until smooth. Set aside.

2. Prepare the cream sauce by adding the water, cream, cashews and white poppy seeds to a blender or food processor and puree until smooth. Set aside.

3. Press the sauté button. Add the blended onion and tomato mixture to the pot. Stir-fry for 7-8 minutes, or until the onion and tomato mixture has thickened. Add the spices and mix well.

4. Pour 1 cup of water into the pot. Place a steamer basket into the pot. Place the eggs on top of the steamer basket. Secure the lid, close the pressure valve and cook for 10 minutes at high pressure.

5. Open the valve to quick release any remaining pressure.

6. Remove the eggs from the steamer basket and place them into a bowl of ice cold water for 5 minutes. Peel the eggs, and make four slits in each egg.

7. Remove the steamer basket from the pressure cooker, and place the eggs into the steel bowl with the cooked tomato sauce. Pour in the cashew cream sauce, press the sauté button and cook for 2-3 minutes, or until the sauce is heated through.

8. Garnish with cilantro and mint and serve.

MEATS

SPICED GROUND
MEAT & RICE

KEEMA PULAO

Serves 4

This one-pot dish of spiced beef and rice is both a weeknight favorite at our house and a dish we serve when we have company. It's flavorful and really quick to make. I'll sometimes leave out the chopped cilantro and mint, but if you want it to taste extra special then don't forget to add the herbs.

1 ½ cups basmati rice,
    soaked for 15-30 minutes

2 tablespoons oil of choice

WHOLE SPICES

5 cardamom pods

4 whole cloves

1 bay leaf

½ cinnamon stick

½ teaspoon cumin seeds

1 pound ground meat of choice

1 onion, diced

5 teaspoons minced garlic

2 teaspoons minced ginger

½ - 1 Serrano pepper
    or green chili, minced,
    adjust to taste

GROUND SPICES

3 teaspoons coriander powder

2 teaspoons paprika

2 teaspoons salt

½ teaspoon black pepper

½ teaspoon garam masala

½ teaspoon turmeric

¼ teaspoon cayenne

2 tomatoes, diced

1 ½ cups water

¼ cup cilantro leaves, chopped

¼ cup mint leaves, chopped

1. Soak the basmati rice in cold water for 15-30 minutes. Drain, rinse and set aside.

2. Press the sauté button, then add the oil to the pot. Allow the oil a minute to heat up, then add the whole spices to the pot and give them a stir. Once the spices begin to sizzle, add the ground meat, onions, garlic, ginger, Serrano pepper and cook until the meat is mostly browned.

3. Add the ground spices, mix well, then add the tomatoes and cook for 5-6 minutes, or until they have softened.

4. Dump the rice on top of the meat (do not mix) then pour water on top. Sprinkle half the cilantro and mint on top of the rice.

5. Secure the lid, close the pressure valve and cook for 6 minutes at high pressure.

6. Naturally release pressure for 10 minutes. Open the valve to release any remaining pressure.

7. Remove whole spices and sprinkle with remaining cilantro and mint.

KERALA GROUND MEAT
COCONUT
CURRY

This Keralite coconut stew is made with meat, potatoes and carrots. I make this often because I almost always have ground meat in my fridge, making this an easy dish to throw together at the last minute. The coconut milk mellows out the flavor, making this a mild curry.

Serves 3-4

2 tablespoons coconut oil

1 teaspoon black mustard seeds

1 onion, diced

1 Serrano pepper or green chili, minced

20 curry leaves

3 teaspoon minced garlic

1 teaspoon minced ginger

SPICES

2 teaspoons meat masala (pg 8)

1 ½ teaspoons salt

1 teaspoon coriander powder

½ teaspoon black pepper

½ teaspoon paprika

½ teaspoon turmeric

1 pound ground meat of choice

3 carrots, chopped

1 potato, chopped

¼ cup water

1 (13.5 ounce) can
   full-fat coconut milk

1.   Press the sauté button, add the coconut oil. Once it melts, add the mustard seeds and when they begin to pop, add the onion, Serrano pepper and curry leaves. Stir-fry for 6-7 minutes, or until the onions begin to brown.

2.   Add the garlic and ginger and stir-fry for 30 seconds. Add the spices, stir, then add the ground meat and cook until it is mostly browned.

3.   Add the carrots, potatoes and ¼ cup water.

4.   Secure the lid, close the pressure valve and cook for 4 minutes at high pressure.

5.   Open the valve to quick release any remaining pressure.

6.   Stir in the coconut milk.

GROUND MEAT
& PEAS

KEEMA MATAR

Serves 3-4

Keema has been one of my favorite dishes since childhood. You can make this with any type of ground meat (beef, lamb and goat are my favorite choices). I typically eat this over rice but you can serve this with flatbread or even use it as a stuffing for samosas (Indian pastries) or parathas (Indian flatbread). I feel like this recipe as well as butter chicken are good "gateway" dishes to Indian cuisine because nearly everyone loves them!

2 tablespoons ghee

1 onion, finely diced

4 teaspoons minced garlic

1 teaspoon minced ginger

1 Serrano pepper or green chili, minced

SPICES

1 tablespoon coriander powder

1 teaspoon paprika

1 teaspoon salt

½ teaspoon black pepper

½ teaspoon ground cumin

½ teaspoon garam masala

½ teaspoon turmeric

¼ teaspoon cayenne

¼ teaspoon ground cardamom

1 pound ground meat of choice

1 (14.5 ounce) can diced tomatoes

2 cups peas

Cilantro, garnish

1.   Press the sauté button, add the ghee and onions and stir-fry for 8-10 minutes, or until the onions begin to brown.

2.   Add the garlic, ginger, Serrano pepper and spices to the pot. Stir-fry for 30 seconds, then add the ground meat and cook until it is mostly browned.

3.   Add the diced tomatoes and peas and mix well

4.   Secure the lid, close the pressure valve and cook for 10 minutes at high pressure.

5.   Open the valve to quick release any remaining pressure.

6.   Press the sauté button to reduce or boil off any extra liquid if needed.

7.   Garnish with cilantro and serve.

LAMB
ROGAN
JOSH

This perfectly cooked lamb will melt in your mouth! The meat is cooked in an onion and yogurt gravy, making it both flavorful and tender. Rogan Josh, a popular Kashmiri dish with Persian origins, is a mild curry that isn't meant to be spicy. The signature red color of this curry traditionally comes from the use of Kashmiri chili peppers, which are very mild and taste similar to paprika. If you want to substitute Kashmiri chili powder for the paprika, feel free to do so.

Serves 4-5

2 tablespoons ghee

2 onions, diced

2 pounds boneless lamb shoulder, cut into 1.5 inch cubes

6 teaspoons minced garlic

2 teaspoons minced ginger

1 bay leaf

SPICES

4 teaspoons paprika

3 teaspoons coriander powder

1 ½ teaspoons salt, adjust to taste

1 teaspoon garam masala

1 teaspoon turmeric

½ teaspoon black pepper

½ teaspoon cinnamon

½ teaspoon ground cardamom

¼ teaspoon ground cumin

⅛ teaspoon ground cloves

1 (15 ounce) can tomato sauce

8 tablespoons yogurt

Cilantro, garnish

1. Press the sauté button and add the ghee to the pot. Once the ghee melts, add the onions and lamb and stir-fry for 6-7 minutes, or until the outside of the lamb pieces are no longer pink.

2. Add the garlic, ginger, bay leaf and spices and give everything a good mix.

3. Add the tomato sauce to the pot and cook for 2-3 minutes. Then stir in the yogurt one tablespoon at a time.

4. Secure the lid, close the pressure valve and cook for 20 minutes at high pressure.

5. Naturally release pressure.

6. Open lid, press the sauté button and cook for 4-5 minutes to boil off some of the liquid and reduce the gravy to a stew like consistency.

7. Garnish with cilantro leaves and serve.

EASY GOAT
CURRY

This goat curry is so easy to make and it's also one of the most popular recipes on my blog. It's a very simple recipe that results in perfectly tender and juicy goat meat that falls right off the bone.

Serves 5-6

2 tablespoons oil of choice

2 pounds bone-in goat pieces (shoulder or leg)

2 onions, diced

3 teaspoons minced garlic

1 ½ teaspoons minced ginger

SPICES

4 whole cloves

4 cardamom pods

1 bay leaf

1 tablespoon coriander powder

2 teaspoons salt, adjust to taste

1 teaspoon ground cumin

1 teaspoon garam masala

1 teaspoon paprika

1 teaspoon turmeric

¼ - ½ teaspoon cayenne, adjust to taste

2 (14.5 ounce) cans diced tomatoes

½ cup water

Cilantro, garnish

1.   Press the sauté button, and add the oil and goat meat to the pot. Once the outside of the meat begins to brown, add the onion, garlic, ginger and spices. Stir-fry for 2-3 minutes.

2.   Pour in the diced tomatoes and water.

3.   Secure the lid, close the pressure valve and cook for 45 minutes at high pressure.

4.   Naturally release pressure.

5.   If you'd like for the dish to have a thicker consistency, press the sauté button to reduce or boil off extra liquid.

6.   Garnish with cilantro.

MALABAR
GOAT PEPPER FRY

Serves 5-6

This goat pepper fry is one of my favorite recipes in the book! I make this for company all the time and everyone raves about how much they like it. This is a dry goat preparation, meaning that the goat pieces are coated in a thick masala sauce rather than swimming in curry. The goat meat is so tender and the spices that cover it make it so flavorful.

3 tablespoons coconut oil, divided

2 onions, diced

1-2 Serrano pepper or green chili, minced

25-30 curry leaves

2 pounds bone-in goat pieces (shoulder or leg)

2 tablespoons minced garlic

2 tablespoons minced ginger

SPICES

1 tablespoon coriander powder

1 tablespoon meat masala (pg 8)

2 teaspoons black pepper

2 teaspoons paprika

2 teaspoons salt

1 teaspoon fennel powder

1 teaspoon turmeric

¼ cup grated coconut*

¼ cup water

1 tablespoon vinegar

1. Press the sauté button and add 2 tablespoons coconut oil to the pot. Once it melts, add the onions, Serrano peppers and curry leaves. Stir-fry for 15 minutes, or until the onions turn brown.

2. Add the goat meat, garlic, ginger and spices. Stir-fry for 4-5 minutes, or until the outside of the meat has browned.

3. Add the grated coconut, water and vinegar.

4. Secure the lid, close the pressure valve and cook for 30 minutes at high pressure.

5. Naturally release pressure.

6. When you open the lid, you will see that the meat has naturally released quite a bit of liquid into the pot. Press the sauté button and cook for 12-15 minutes, adding the remaining 1 tablespoon of coconut oil at about the halfway mark. The consistency of the dish should be mostly dry. The goat meat should be coated with a thick masala sauce.

Find frozen unsweetened grated coconut at your local Indian grocery store.

70

KERALA
BEEF FRY

ERACHI ULARTHIYATHU

Serves 5-6

This recipe is a Christian Keralite dish called Erachi Ularthiyathu, which just means "beef fry" and it is my husband's all-time favorite recipe. I used to only make it on special occasions, because it took a lot of time to make but ever since adapting it to be a one-pot dish, I make it more often. Like the goat pepper fry, this Kerala beef fry is also considered a dry curry. The spices coat the tender and juicy pieces of beef stew meat. You can add as many green chilies as you'd like to this dish. If it were up to Roby, he'd add 10 but we "compromise" by adding 2.

3 tablespoons coconut oil, divided

1 teaspoon black mustard seeds

1 red onion, sliced

1 red onion, finely chopped

2 Serrano peppers or green chilies, slit lengthwise but still intact

35-40 curry leaves

¼ cup chopped garlic

¼ cup chopped ginger

SPICES

1 tablespoon meat masala (pg 8)

2 teaspoons coriander powder

1 teaspoon salt

1 teaspoon turmeric

½ teaspoon black pepper

½ teaspoon cayenne

2 pounds beef stew meat

½ cup coconut slices*

2 tablespoons fresh lemon juice

*Find frozen coconut meat/slices at your local Indian grocery store.

1.   Press the sauté button. Add 2 tablespoons of coconut oil and the mustard seeds to the pot. Once the seeds begin to splutter, add the onions, Serrano peppers and curry leaves. Stir-fry for 15 minutes or until the onions turn brown.

2.   Add the garlic, ginger and spices. Stir-fry for 30 seconds, then add the beef, coconut slices and lemon juice. Stir-fry for 5-6 minutes to brown the beef on all sides.

3.   Secure the lid, close the pressure valve and cook for 35 minutes at high pressure.

4.   Naturally release pressure.

5.   When you open the lid, you will see that the meat has naturally released quite a bit of liquid into the pot. Press the sauté button and cook for 15-18 minutes, adding the remaining 1 tablespoon of coconut oil at about the halfway mark. Stir-fry the beef until it is mostly dry, coated in masala and dark brown.

PORK VINDALOO

Serves 5-6

Vindaloo is known as a popular Goan curry, but it is actually of Portuguese origin. The dish was brought to India by explorers where the recipe was adapted using local ingredients and spices. This spicy curry calls for vinegar, which adds a tangy flavor to the stew. I recommend using pork shoulder in this recipe because it results in tender and juicy meat.

4 tablespoons oil of choice

1 teaspoon cumin seeds

½ teaspoon black mustard seeds

2 onions, diced

1 Serrano pepper or green chili, minced

2 pounds pork shoulder,
    cut into 1.5 inch cubes

3 tablespoons minced garlic

1 tablespoon minced ginger

SPICES

4 teaspoons paprika

2 teaspoons salt

1 teaspoon coriander powder

½ teaspoon cinnamon

½ teaspoon ground cardamom

½ teaspoon black pepper

¼ - ½ teaspoon cayenne

4 tablespoons white vinegar

¾ cup water

Cilantro, garnish

1. Press the sauté button, add oil and allow it a minute to heat up. Add the cumin and mustard seeds. Once the cumin seeds brown and the mustard seeds begin to pop, add the onions and Serrano pepper. Stir-fry for 8-10 minutes, or until the onions begin to brown.

2. Add the pork, garlic and ginger. Stir for 3-4 minutes to brown the meat on all sides.

3. Add the spices, give everything a good mix, then add the vinegar and water.

4. Secure the lid, close the pressure valve and cook for 25 minutes at high pressure.

5. Naturally release pressure.

6. Open lid, press the sauté button and cook for 8-10 minutes to boil off some of the liquid and reduce the gravy to a stew like consistency.

7. Garnish with cilantro and serve.

DESSERTS

CHAI FOR ONE
OR
CHAI FOR A PARTY

You might be wondering why anyone would make chai in a pressure cooker. It can be faster to make it on a stovetop, especially a single cup. But when you make it in a pressure cooker, there's no need to babysit the tea. You can set it and forget it. I always use my pressure cooker when making chai for friends or for a large party because it's such a hands off recipe. I also like making chai for myself and my husband everyday before work. I can prepare the tea, get ready for the day, then come downstairs to a fresh cup of steaming hot chai.

CHAI FOR 1

½ cup water

1 black tea bag

1 cardamom pod, lightly crushed

1 whole clove

Pinch of fennel seeds
  (approx. ⅛ teaspoon)

½ cup milk

Sweetener, adjust to taste

CHAI FOR 4

2 cups water

4 black tea bags

4 cardamom pods, lightly crushed

4 whole cloves

½ teaspoon fennel seeds

2 cups milk

Sweetener, adjust to taste

CHAI FOR 10

5 cups water

10 black tea bags

10 cardamom pods, lightly crushed

10 whole cloves

1 ¼ teaspoons fennel seeds

5 cups milk

Sweetener, adjust to taste

1. Multiply the ingredients according to the number of people drinking chai.

2. Press the sauté button and add water, black tea, cardamom pods, cloves and fennel seeds to the pot. Once the water begins to steam, pour the milk into the pot (make sure the water is steaming before adding the milk as this will prevent the milk from burning at the bottom of the pot).

3. Secure the lid, close the pressure valve and cook for 2 minutes at high pressure.

4. Naturally release pressure for 15 minutes. Open the valve to release any remaining pressure.

5. Add sweetener to taste, then serve.

CARROT
PUDDING

GAJAR KA HALWA

Serves 4

This classic Indian dessert has been my dad's favorite sweet since childhood. He knows good halwa and he loves this recipe. My dad actually helped me come up with the method for making this delicious, rich halwa. He taught me a couple secrets to making this recipe: 1. Wait to add the ghee until after you pressure cook the carrots as that helps give the halwa that desired dark orange/red color. 2. You don't need to use a lot of milk to make this dessert but don't cut back on the ghee.

1 pound carrots, grated
   (approx. 4 cups)

½ cup whole milk
   or full-fat coconut milk

¼ cup water

½ cup sugar

4 tablespoons ghee

⅛ teaspoon ground cardamom

Chopped pistachios
   or other nut, garnish

1. Add the carrots, milk and water to the pot. Secure the lid, close the pressure valve and cook for 1 minute at high pressure.

2. Open the valve to quick release any remaining pressure.

3. Press sauté and add the sugar. Stir for 6-7 minutes, or until most of the liquid has reduced. Then, add the ghee and stir-fry the carrots for another 6-7 minutes, or until the carrots become dry and the ghee separates from the mixture. The carrots should look dark orange/reddish in color.

4. Add the cardamom, mix well, then garnish with chopped nuts.

I don't use khoya when I make halwa, but if you'd like to use it, feel free to mix it in at the end when adding cardamom powder.

If you are making this for a dinner party, serve a small portion of halwa with a large scoop of ice cream.

If you want to make this dairy-free, you can use full-fat coconut milk and coconut oil instead of ghee (but it won't taste quite as good).

CREAMY **CARDAMOM** RICE PUDDING

KHEER

Serves 4-6

Kheer, a creamy rice pudding, is one of my favorite desserts to make and eat. It requires just a few essential ingredients: rice, milk and sugar. I almost always have those three ingredients at my house. You can serve this dessert at any temperature and it'll taste good. When the weather is cold, I prefer to serve warm kheer, but if it's hot out, then I like to serve it chilled.

¼ cup basmati rice,
   soaked for 15-30 minutes

½ cup water

3 cups whole milk or full-fat coconut milk

½ cup sugar, adjust to taste

½ teaspoon ground cardamom,
   adjust to taste

Pinch of saffron

Crushed nuts, (pistachios, almonds, or
   cashews), garnish

Golden Raisins, garnish

1.   Soak the basmati rice in cold water for 15-30 minutes. Drain, rinse and set aside.

2.   Press the sauté button and add ½ cup water to the pot. Once the water begins to steam, pour the milk into the pot. (Make sure the water is steaming before adding the milk as this will prevent the milk from burning at the bottom of the pot.) Add the rice, stir.

3.   Secure the lid, close the pressure valve and cook for 20 minutes at high pressure.

4.   Naturally release pressure.

5.   Press sauté. Add the sugar, cardamom and saffron to the pot. Stir until well combined. The kheer will thicken as it cools. If you prefer a thicker pudding, press sauté and stir until desired consistency.

6.   Serve this dessert hot, warm, cold or at room temperature. Garnish with toppings (nuts and raisins) prior to serving.

SWEET SAFFRON
FRUIT & NUT
RICE

MEETHE CHAWAL

Serves 6-7

This sweetly spiced saffron and cardamom flavored rice is a well-known Punjabi dessert. While my mom makes a lot of different desserts, I always think of meethe chawal as her signature dish. She has been making this sweetly spiced pulao on special occasions for as long as I can remember and it is always a hit with guests. This dish is traditionally yellow in color and while many cooks choose to add yellow food coloring to their meethe chawal for presentation purposes, I always leave it out. Feel free to add it though if you'd like! For a variation to this dish, try topping the rice with sweet (canned) mandarins.

2 cups basmati rice,
   soaked for 1 hour

2 tablespoons ghee

WHOLE SPICES

10 whole cloves

5 green cardamom

1 black cardamom

1 bay leaf

½ stick cinnamon

1 tablespoon raisins

2 cups water

Pinch of saffron

ADD LATER

2 cups ripe pineapple chunks
   or 1 (20 ounce) can of
   pineapple chunks, drained

1 cup grated coconut*

1 teaspoon lemon juice

2 tablespoons water

1 ½ cups sugar

¼ cup chopped pistachios
   or nuts of choice, garnish

*Find frozen unsweetened grated coconut at your local Indian grocery store.

1.   Soak the basmati rice in cold water for 1 hour. Drain, rinse and set aside.

2.   Press the sauté button, then add the ghee. Once the ghee melts, add the whole spices to the pot. As soon as the spices begin to sizzle, add the raisins and give them a stir, then add the rice, water and saffron.

3.   Secure the lid, close the pressure valve and cook for 7 minutes at high pressure.

4.   Open the valve to quick release any remaining pressure.

5.   Add the pineapple chunks, grated coconut, lemon juice, 2 tablespoons of water and mix well. Carefully pour the sugar on top of the rice, making sure it doesn't get on the edges of the steel pot. Do not mix the sugar into the rice.

6.   Secure the lid, close the pressure valve and cook for 1 minute at high pressure.

7.   Naturally release pressure.

8.   Mix well, garnish with chopped pistachios and serve.

STEAMED
RICE CAKE

VATTAYAPPAM

Serves 6-7

This is a popular tea-time snack in Kerala. To make this cake, you must first ferment the batter and then steam it. The result: a perfectly soft, slightly spongy rice cake. I tested this recipe dozens of times before finally coming up with this method that results in a perfectly cooked cake. While this cake does require some preparation, if you follow the steps as they're written then you'll see it's actually not that difficult to make. I recommend making and eating this on the same day as that's when it tastes the best. You can also leave the sugar out of this recipe and make a steamed savory cake that you can serve with any Keralite curry.

1 cup basmati rice,
   soak for 4-5 hours

3 tablespoons warm water

½ teaspoon active dry yeast

1 tablespoon sugar

¾ cup cold water

½ cup grated coconut*

Coconut oil for greasing cake pan

ADD LATER

¼ cup sugar

¼ teaspoon ground cardamom

1 tablespoon raisins, fried in ghee

1 tablespoon cashews, fried in ghee

*Freshly grated coconut isn't always practical. I suggest buying frozen unsweetened grated coconut at your local Indian grocery store. I thaw the coconut before measuring it.

1.   Soak the rice in cold water for 4-5 hours. Drain, rinse and set aside.

2.   To prepare the cake batter, you will first need to bloom the yeast. To do this, place the 3 tablespoons of water, yeast and sugar in a small bowl. Allow it to rest for a few minutes or until it blooms and becomes frothy. This step is important. If the yeast doesn't froth at the top, then it's likely dead and you will need to buy new yeast.

3.   While you wait for the yeast to bloom, prepare the pressure cooker by adding 2 cups of water to the steel pot. Place the wire rack that came with your pressure cooker into the pot.

4.   Add the drained rice and ¾ cup cold water to a blender and blend until mostly smooth (coarsely ground rice is also fine). Add the grated coconut and the bowl of frothy yeast into the blender and blend again until well combined.

5.   Pour this batter into an oven-safe bowl and set the bowl on top of the trivet inside the steel inner pot.

6.   Secure the lid, close the pressure valve, press the yogurt button and set the time for 2 hours. When the time is up, remove the lid and you should see that the batter has fermented and has doubled in size.

7.   Remove the bowl of batter, add an additional 1 cup of water into the inner pot then place an empty well-greased 7.5 inch cake pan on top of the trivet. Press the sauté button to heat up the water and the empty pan.

8.   Add ¼ cup sugar and cardamom to the batter and mix until well combined.

9.   Pour the batter into the now hot cake pan that is sitting in the steel inner pot. Sprinkle cashews and raisins on top of the batter. Lightly cover the cake pan with a piece of foil.

10. Secure the lid, close the pressure valve, press the steam button and set the time for 30 minutes at high pressure.

11. Naturally release pressure. Remove the hot cake pan out of the pot and place it on a wire rack to cool.

BUTTERNUT SQUASH PUDDING

BUTTERNUT SQUASH HALWA

Serves 2-3

This is a very rich halwa and so while I say that it serves 2-3, you can easily serve it to a family of four by adding some ice cream to go along with it. I usually buy pre-cut butternut squash from the grocery store as it makes this an even easier dessert to make.

1 pound peeled and chopped
  butternut squash

1 tablespoon ghee

5 tablespoons sugar,
  adjust to taste

½ teaspoon ground cardamom

¼ cup slivered almonds
  or chopped nut of choice, garnish

1. To prepare the squash, add 2 cups water into the steel inner pot, then place a steamer basket into the pot. Place the peeled and cut squash in the basket, then secure the lid, close the pressure valve, press the steam button and set the time for 15 minutes at high pressure.

2. Open the valve to quick release any remaining pressure.

3. Remove the squash and steamer basket from the pot. Set the squash aside.

4. Dump out any water still remaining in the bottom of the pot, then press the sauté button and add the ghee and the squash. Mash the soft squash with a spoon, then add sugar and cardamom. Stir-fry for 3-4 minutes, or until the halwa turns a shade darker and the ghee releases a nutty aroma.

5. Garnish with crushed nuts and serve.

SWEET LENTILS
IN COCONUT MILK

KERALA STYLE
MOONG DAL PAYASAM

Serves 5-6

Sweetened lentils are the star of this simple dessert. The name of the South Indian state of Kerala translates to "the land of coconut trees," and so it's no surprise that this traditional moong dal payasam calls for coconut milk. There, they use fresh coconut milk of course, but for simplicity's sake, my recipe calls for canned coconut milk. If you've ever had kheer before, then you'll find that this is a similar dessert, but made with lentils instead of rice and coconut milk instead of milk.

½ cup small yellow lentils (moong dal)

1 tablespoon ghee

¼ cup cashews, halved

¼ cup coconut slices*

1 ¼ cups water

ADD LATER

1 cup coconut sugar or jaggery, adjust to taste

½ teaspoon ground cardamom

1 (13.5 ounce) can of full-fat coconut milk

1.   Press the sauté button. Add the small yellow lentils (moong dal). Dry roast the dal for 2-3 minutes, or until it turns golden and gives off a slightly nutty aroma. Remove the lentils and rinse them under cold water.

2.   Press the sauté button. Add ghee to the pot. Once it melts, add the cashews and coconut pieces. Stir-fry until golden. Remove and set aside.

3.   Add the rinsed lentils back into the pot along with 1 ¼ cups water. Secure the lid, close the pressure valve and cook for 12 minutes at high pressure.

4.   Naturally release pressure.

5.   Mash the lentils with a ladle, then press the sauté button, add the coconut sugar and cardamom and mix well. Pour in the coconut milk and stir until well combined. Cook for 2-3 minutes, or until it thickens a bit.

6.   Serve warm or cold and garnish with the ghee coated cashews and coconut pieces.

Find frozen coconut slices at your local Indian grocery store.

SWEET AND SOUR GREEN MANGO
COOLER

AAM KA PANNA

Serves 6-7

This green mango cooler is so refreshing! It's the drink you're going to want to make during a heat wave. Think of it as the Indian version of lemonade, only instead of lemons, this recipe calls for another sour fruit: unripe green mangoes. This recipe also calls for a few spices: roasted cumin powder, black salt and salt. The first two spices are very unique in flavor and can be overpowering if you've never had them before. I suggest adding a small amount at first. If you're like my family though, then you'll probably sprinkle even more black salt on top!

2 unripe green mangoes (1½ pounds total)

4 cups water

½ cup sugar, adjust to taste

½ teaspoon black salt, adjust to taste

½ teaspoon roasted cumin powder (pg 8), adjust to taste

¼ teaspoon salt

Ice cubes

Fresh mint, garnish

1.   Using a knife, make several small slits in the mangoes.

2.   Add 2 cups water into the steel inner pot, then place a steamer basket or the wire rack that came with the pressure cooker into the pot. Place the green mangoes on top of the rack.

3.   Secure the lid, close the pressure valve and cook for 15 minutes at high pressure.

4.   Open the valve to quick release any remaining pressure.

5.   Allow the mangoes to cool down, then remove the peel. Place the pulp into a blender along with the 4 cups of water, sugar, black salt, roasted cumin powder and salt and blend until smooth. Taste the drink and add more spices according to taste.

6.   Pour this drink into glasses filled with ice. Sprinkle a little roasted cumin powder on top if desired and garnish with a fresh sprig of mint.

You may need to adjust the cooking time depending on the size of the mangoes.

82

Printed in Great Britain
by Amazon